YAMAHA
THE NEW DAWN
ISLE OF MAN TT™ 1961–1981

YAMAHA
THE NEW DAWN

ISLE OF MAN TT™ 1961–1981

MATTHEW RICHARDSON

AN IMPRINT OF PEN & SWORD BOOKS LTD.
YORKSHIRE – PHILADELPHIA

First published in Great Britain in 2025 by
Pen and Sword Transport
An imprint of
Pen & Sword Books Ltd.
Yorkshire - Philadelphia

Copyright © Matthew Richardson, 2025

ISBN 978 1 39907 969 3

The right of Matthew Richardson to be identified as author of this work has been asserted by him in accordance with the Copyright, Designs and Patents Act 1988.

A CIP catalogue record for this book is available from the British Library.

All rights reserved. No part of this book may be reproduced, transmitted, downloaded, decompiled or reverse engineered in any form or by any means, electronic or mechanical including photocopying, recording or by any information storage and retrieval system, without permission from the Publisher in writing. No part of this book may be used or reproduced in any manner for the purpose of training artificial intelligence technologies or systems.

Typeset in INDIA by IMPEC eSolutions
Printed and bound in the England by CPI Group (UK) Ltd, Croydon, CR0 4YY

The Publisher's authorised representative in the EU for product safety is Authorised Rep Compliance Ltd., Ground Floor, 71 Lower Baggot Street, Dublin D02 P593, Ireland.
www.arccompliance.com

For a complete list of Pen & Sword titles please contact

PEN & SWORD BOOKS LIMITED
47 Church Street, Barnsley, South Yorkshire, S70 2AS, England
E-mail: enquiries@pen-and-sword.co.uk
Website: www.pen-and-sword.co.uk

or

PEN AND SWORD BOOKS
1950 Lawrence Rd, Havertown, PA 19083, USA
E-mail: uspen-and-sword@casematepublishers.com
Website: www.penandswordbooks.com

CONTENTS

Foreword	6
Acknowledgements	7
Introduction	9
Chapter One Turning the Tide, 1961–1965	17
Chapter Two Who Wears the Crown? 1966–1968	42
Chapter Three The Age of the Privateer, 1969–1973	63
Chapter Four The TZ Years, 1974–1981	90
Chapter Five Sidecar Success, 1974–1981	133
Epilogue	151
Notes	153
Bibliography	157
Index	158

FOREWORD

There is no doubt that the history and success of Yamaha, in both the music and motorcycle industries, is indeed a fascinating one. The amount of the research that Matthew Richardson has put into this excellent book is formidable. I would class it as one of those books that you don't want to put down, as you really want to know what happened next and particularly why and how in 1955 the Yamaha Motor Company was formed.

I guess I was lucky enough to be one of those riders who benefitted so much from the availability of the over the counter Yamaha racing machinery in the early 1970s through to the mid-1980s. Having said that, although I must have ridden many different both race and production Yamaha machines from 125 to 750cc throughout my career, I never actually owned one until after my retirement from the sport! My association with the brand began in 1970 and quite recently both at the Manx Grand Prix and the BSB round at Donington Park I took part in parades.

You'd never guess what I was riding!

Charlie Williams
Nine Times Isle of Man TT Winner

ACKNOWLEDGMENTS

Some time ago, I wrote a book which charted the arrival (and ultimate dominance) at the Isle of Man TT races of the Honda Motor Company. Subsequently I felt that it would be an interesting proposition to explore events 'from the other side of the fence', as experienced by one of their greatest rivals, Yamaha. I am therefore grateful to Pen and Sword Books for allowing me the opportunity to do just that.

Once more I would like to extend my warmest thanks to my great friend Ted Macauley for his unstinting support and encouragement with this book. Yet again, Ted allowed me to quote from his own work, in particular *Yamaha: The Legend*. Ted had a front row seat for the titanic motorcycle racing battles of the 1960s and was on first name terms with Mike Hailwood, Jim Redman, Phil Read and a host of other legendary figures. As always Ted, I hope that this meets your eye.

Legendary TT racer Mick Grant kindly allowed me to quote material from his book, *Takin' the Mick*, covering his years with Yamaha machinery, for which I also thank him. Likewise, multiple TT winner Charlie Williams was more than generous in sharing with me memories of his racing years, as well as material from his own book, for which I am sincerely grateful. Charlie was also kind enough to contribute the foreword, and this seal of approval means a great deal to me.

As so often before, I wish to express my gratitude to the late Ken Sprayson, who so generously allowed me to use photographs from his personal collection. In the 1970s Ken always seemed to be in just the right place and at the right time to capture a classic image. Bill Snelling at Fottofinders/TTracepics again helped me with photos, and I thank him warmly for this.

Wendy Thirkettle at Manx National Heritage assisted me with picture research, and I thank her for this contribution. Acknowledgement is made to MNH for use of the image of Taneharu Noguchi herein.

Likewise, my thanks go to Simon Crellin at the Isle of Man Government Motorsport Office for assistance with use of the TT trademark.

Logos, model names and designations, where they have been used in this book, have been so solely for the purposes of identification, illustration and decoration and remain the property of the trademark holder. Any errors of fact or interpretation are entirely my own.

Matthew Richardson
Douglas, 2023

INTRODUCTION

The origins of the Yamaha Motor Company are reflected in its logo, which shows three tuning forks. The firm began as a musical instrument manufacturer, and the Yamaha Corporation (known originally as Nippon Gakki Corporation) was founded by Torakusu Yamaha in Hamamatsu in 1887, specifically to manufacture reed organs and pianos. He came of age in the 1860s and 1870s, a time when Japan was rapidly opening up to Western ideas and technology, after many years of feudalism and isolation. His father was an astronomer, and this led to an early interest in mechanical things; later he became apprenticed to an English watchmaker. He also developed an interest in medical equipment, but it was only at the age of 35, when he moved to Hamamatsu, that he first came into contact with the musical instruments which would define his career. After being asked to repair a school organ, he realised that he could manufacture the components himself. His first efforts were poor, but he persevered and soon started to receive orders for his products. He employed cabinet makers and joiners to assist him in building his instruments, and the first factory was located in an abandoned temple. An early version of the company logo showed a Chinese phoenix, holding a tuning fork in its beak. By the beginning of the twentieth century, Yamaha had become the largest manufacturer of musical instruments in Japan.

However its progress was not always smooth. In 1916 Torakusu Yamaha died at the age of 64. The empire that he had established was taken over by a new president, Chiyomaru Amano. At first, things continued to improve under his watch, and a branch factory was established at Hokkaido to take advantage of plentiful wood supplies in that area. This led to the creation of a harmonica factory, employing 600 women, as the First World War produced a temporary sales boom. However this was not to last, as with the ending of the war the German Mark collapsed in value, resulting in large quantities of cheap German-made pianos and harmonicas being imported into Japan by rival companies. To add to the company's woes the 1923 Tokyo earthquake burned down the branch there, at great financial cost, and in 1926 workers went on strike for improved pay. Some 350 workers were laid off, and all work was halted for over 100 days, but Amano refused to concede anything to the strikers.

Eventually he was replaced by a new president, Kaichi Kawakami. He was more in the mould of Torakusu Yamaha, and a brilliant and greatly respected engineer. A graduate of Tokyo University, he gladly accepted the massive responsibility thrust on to his shoulders: he certainly did not want to see workers being pushed out of the company, and he immediately stressed his readiness to shoulder whatever responsibilities were necessary in order to reinvigorate the firm, pay off its crippling debts, restore good industrial relations and end the long drawn-out strike. His words at that time were an apt demonstration of his determination to carry on the good works established by the company's late lamented founder, Torakusu Yamaha:

> The underlying motive that led me to accept this position is that the work of Nippon Gakki is not just that of a business interested only in profits. I have prepared myself to make sacrifices to realise the need for adjustment and

to rationalise the company and I pledge to devote all my energies toward this end ... I make a solemn oath to all employees that I want to make this company a good one. I call upon you to co-operate in a united effort to make it a company par excellence so that in the future we will earn admiration and trust the world over for the products of Nippon Gakki.[1]

The company was contracted to manufacture wooden, and later metal aeroplane propellers by the Japanese government during the Second World War, but like many other Japanese companies, it struggled in the aftermath of the country's defeat. It had become heavily dependent on war contracts which had abruptly ended, Japan had been severely bombed, its infrastructure had mostly been destroyed and there were now many restrictions as a result of Allied occupation of the country. The president by this point was in poor health, but had been grooming his son, Gen-Ichi, to take over the reins. Like his father he was an extremely able man. In the early 1950s, new chairman Gen-Ichi Kawakami decided to repurpose Yamaha's now underutilised war-time facilities, to manufacture small motorcycles for leisure use. He created an entity separate from the parent firm for this purpose, and named it Yamaha Motor Company. Today the two are entirely distinct, though on the stock market the parent, Yamaha Corporation, still holds the largest private share of the automotive company.

Yamaha Motor Company was incorporated on 1 July 1955, and its first product, a single-cylinder 125cc two-stroke motorcycle, was a copy of a German DKW machine. It was called the YA-1, and nicknamed Akatombo, the 'Red Dragonfly'. With a maroon framework and cream tank sides, as well as telescopic front forks and an oil damper system, it was the first motorcycle to carry the symbol of the triple tuning fork. Racing success came almost immediately with victory in the 125cc class in the Mount Fuji Ascent. The newest of the factories bidding for a place in the epic sales battle that was then ongoing in the Japanese home market, Yamaha entered several YA-1 specials in the race – and then proceeded to stun the opposition by winning it outright. Few people at Asama had realised the strength of their challenge – until it was too late. The YA-1 quickly became a prized possession. To the hundreds of young motorcycle enthusiasts, who were being tempted on all sides, it had proved itself as a true race winner.

Yamaha proved it was no fluke by also sweeping the podium with first, second and third place in the All Japan Autobike Endurance Road Race the same year. The YA-1 was followed by the YA-2 of 1957, another 125cc two-stroke, but this time with significantly improved frame and suspension. The YD-1 of 1957 was a 250cc two-stroke twin-cylinder motorcycle, resembling the YA-2, but with a larger and more powerful motor. A performance version of this bike, the YDS-1 housed the 250cc two-stroke twin in a double downtube cradle frame and offered the first five-speed transmission in a Japanese motorcycle.

That year, Kawakami gave a speech to his employees in which he explained the motives behind such a seemingly incongruous move from the manufacture of musical instruments to that of motorcycles. The reasons are intriguing in themselves, but Kawakami's speech also gives a fascinating insight into that particular mix of commercial aggression and paternalistic concern for employees that has always characterised the Yamaha organisation:

> The musical instrument industry is considered to be somewhat restricted in materials and scope, and can be

expected to face difficulties in the future. We at Nippon Gakki cannot remain passive, assuming the responsibility for a large number of people just on the basis of present-day good business. Unless management, as part of its responsibility, conducts research to determine possible future business activities, at a time when adequate financial reserves are at hand, it will not be able to take any necessary drastic action when some day there prove to be more workers than work. Nippon Gakki must look forward to tomorrow's business activity whilst today's business is still expanding ...

The company had considered entering the fields of sewing machines and scooters, but both were already over produced. Then it had considered making automotive parts, but life as a subcontractor was precarious and they would always be at the mercy of the motor manufacturer, and of their success or failure. Instead, Yamaha would produce finished units:

> The outcome of the above thought-process is that we consider the possibility of motor cycle production to be our best opportunity for success, even though the best point of entry might already have passed us by. As a result of information gained from Mr Takei, the chief of our research section, who has undertaken a study tour of the major motor cycle manufacturing facilities in Japan, we were able to take the view that we could survive in the motorcycle field, despite our late entry and the existing manufacturers.[2]

He added that it should not be thought that motorcycles were merely a sideline or some sort of corporate hobby, but that it was a carefully thought out move, made in the best interests of the company. He went on to admit however that there were those who, at the time, counselled strongly against it.

Yamaha made its first tentative steps in international competition in 1958, when it entered the Catalina Grand Prix, Los Angeles, again with the YA-1. The highest placed machine finished sixth, ridden by Fumio Itoh, who would go on to enjoy Isle of Man TT fame, but the race was difficult, with only eleven of the thirty-two riders that started completing the distance. After moving up from last place to sixth, Ito drew a great deal of attention locally for his riding skills. Yamaha subsequently took part in a half-mile track race in Los Angeles, where it claimed victory. The exploits of the Yamaha team, which had made the long journey all the way from Japan, captivated the local media and provided substantial momentum for the entry of Yamaha motorcycles into the US market.

The next year, in August 1959, Yamaha set up a factory motorcycle development team at the Hamamatsu Research Laboratory. While it was not an official organisation, it was the first time that a specialised racing development team had been assembled. It consisted of groups assigned to engine design, performance development, chassis performance, road testing, and other areas. Spurred on by rivalry with other firms such as Honda, the groups committed all their energy to developing machines capable of winning in the road racing World Championship, Yamaha's ultimate ambition. Hiroshi Naito, later to be appointed to the board as head of motorcycle technology, was put in charge of research and development; another expert, Noriyuki Hata, was invited to join the company. Naito stated:

> We wanted to get our machines abroad as quickly as we could. Grand Prix success was necessary to bolster sales.

Efforts were concentrated on a two-stroke 250 cc racing model – the RD48 – based on the abundant technical data we had collected through our successful experience in national racing. The RD48 was later further developed into the RD56.

The second weapon in the Yamaha armoury was the 125cc YX18. That was Hata's project. He explained: 'I got my job with Yamaha in 1959 and my first task was to develop a 125 cc racer. Ever since I have been concentrating on this line of work.'[3]

That same year, Honda had made the first foray into this world when they appeared at the Isle of Man TT races. They were received with bemused curiosity by the locals, who found both riders and mechanics equally mysterious. They spoke a language almost no one could understand, and seemed to have an extraordinary work ethic, toiling around the clock in immaculate overalls and white gloves. Yet what hardly anyone realised was that this was just the vanguard of a wave of Japanese factories who were about to break into Grand Prix racing, and which would come to dominate the 1960s and 1970s.

In a bid to further his knowledge, in 1960 Naito flew to Europe to observe Western racing machines in action. The lightweight classes were dominated by MV Agusta and MZ, the two-stroke machines of the latter were incredibly fast but in their battles with the former were usually let down by reliability problems. None the less Naito never lost faith in two-stroke technology and its potential, and believed it could be successful if these problems could be overcome. Unlike Soichiro Honda, who was utterly wedded to four-stroke technology and stuck with it throughout the 1960s, those at Yamaha firmly upheld the principle of the two-stroke engine. Their conviction was based mainly on the simple fact that there are fewer moving parts than in four-stroke engines, and that the power impulses are delivered at twice the rate. The recurring problem with two-strokes however has always been the Achilles Heel of the petrol-oil mixture. Yamaha's answer was the auto-lube system. This constantly metered the amount of oil fed to the engine, in accordance with rev speed and throttle opening. It was to be the first pressure-lubrication device to be fitted on a production model after it had been used in racing machinery. The system was thorough; the build-up of carbon deposits and spark plug fouling was reduced drastically and exhaust fumes cut right down.

It is a little-known detail that the first appearance by a Yamaha machine at the Isle of Man TT was not in 1961, as frequently appears in print. In fact, the previous year, 35-year-old American rider Samuel 'Sonny' Angel from National City, California had entered a 250cc factory tuned machine, though he was a non-starter in the Lightweight race.

By 1961, at last Yamaha was ready to enter a World Championship Grand Prix road race. Following Taneharu Noguchi's eighth place result in the 125cc class in the company's debut appearance, the French Grand Prix, he went on to finish seventeenth in the Ultra-Lightweight category, whilst Fumio Itoh went on to capture sixth place in the 250cc Lightweight class at that year's Isle of Man TT races, which Yamaha took part in for the first time. These results constituted the company's first steps on the Grand Prix stage, and foreshadowed even greater things to come.

Chapter One

1961–1965
TURNING THE TIDE

For the 1961 season Yamaha arrived in Europe with the RA41. It had a single expansion chamber that was both thin and short – the Yamaha engineers insisted that a 125cc machine need not use two cylinders. The double cradle frame was made of molybdenum chromium steel and there was a telescopic front fork, with spring exposed. The rear swing arm type had a damper located quite close to the swing arm centre – a design that the company had seen used on the Suzuki moto cross model. Its main characteristic was that the cushion stroke could be made longer, but the spring was finely pitched for pliable setting. The brakes were leading-trailing type with 260mm diameter double panels mounted on the front and a one-sided leading-trailing type on the rear. Both had big air scoops. For the Isle of Man TT, the RA41 was fitted with a special cowling, or fairing, that completely enclosed the handlebars. The team also brought some RD48 machines, in which the two-stroke air-cooled two-cylinder engine used gasoline-oil mixed fuel, while also mounting an oil pump-powered forced lubrication system. It also featured rotary disc valves on either side of the crankshaft and a carburettor with separate float chamber. This power unit, with its output of 35PS, was mounted in a double cradle type frame. The chassis was styled after the Italian production racers of the day in terms of the type of rear suspension mounting and the elliptical cross-section of the rear arm. Its look was defined by the full cowling that covered even the handlebars, which was later revised for the final round of the season, the Argentinian Grand Prix. The 'R' in its RD48 designation stood for racer and the 'D' was Yamaha's designation for the 250cc class ('A' was the designation for 125cc machines). The '48' was the development code for the engine, which derived from the YX48.

Among the Yamaha riders was Hideo Oishi from Hamamatsu, who had previously raced in Japan only. Itoh had been present at the previous year's TT with a BMW, though he had been a non-starter in the Senior race in 1960. A crash during practice saw Osamu Masuko taken to hospital with concussion, lacerations of the face and a broken thumb. He was replaced in the team by Guatemalan Luis Giron. Although Gary Hocking dominated the 250cc class in practice, Itoh, the fastest of the Yamaha riders gave a creditable performance.

In the 125cc race on 12 June 1961 Mike Hailwood dominated proceedings, leading from start to finish. Yoshikasa Sunako, who had placed sixth in the Unites States Grand Prix earlier in the year, dropped out after Sulby Straight when his engine cut out. Itoh retired at Quarter Bridge, whilst Taneharu Noguchi, the 27-year-old sales manager of the Nomuro Motor Company, from Tokyo, Japan finished seventeenth. Itoh's sixth spot in the 250cc race was offset somewhat by his team mate Sunako's second retirement of the meeting.

Yamaha might have been forgiven for feeling totally downcast after their experiences on the Isle of Man in 1961, but when they left the Island for Holland and Belgium, they were determined to do well in the next World Championship rounds, even in the face of such total domination by Honda. Their experience had been painful and, at times, embarrassing.

But they learned both from their own mistakes and from the successes of their rivals.

The engineering staff had already managed to work some improvements into the machines, but they realised quite quickly that they still needed some extra speed and reliability. Both the 125 and the 250cc had been troubled by plugs oiling, shocking vibration, carburation problems, and a shortfall on power and durability. The engineers were pressed into an exhaustive programme of development in preparation for the 1962 season. In the event, Yamaha's assault on the World Championships of 1962 stuttered to a halt as a result of the domestic recession which followed the settlement of the Korean issue, and there was no Yamaha presence on the Isle of Man for that year's TT races. Their target now became 1963. They built another 125cc, the RA55, and developed the RD48 into the rather more sophisticated RD56. At last, Yamaha were turning the corner, and other Japanese manufacturers began to fear the threat they posed.

In 1963 Naito once again took a team to Europe. They had a brand new RA75 and the sensationally fast RD56, even further developed after its run-out against the Hondas and Suzukis in Japan only a few months before. Hata was the chief engineer, controlling two other engineers and five mechanics. There was the usual money manager, that unique institution among Japanese teams abroad, and five riders, all Japanese, the by now regular line-up of Itoh, Sunako, Masuko, Oishi and Hasegawa. The programme, still modest by anybody's standards, was to compete for the prizes at the Isle of Man, Holland and Belgium, and at home at the Suzuka circuit, the setting for the end of season Japanese Grand Prix.

Before the party set off for the Isle of Man, Itoh flew to the United States to take part in a short series of international meetings which would act as a warm up for the forthcoming Grand Prix events and to test the capabilities of the RD56, which would soon prove itself to be the fastest 250cc machine in the world. He took two wins, one in a straight 250cc event and another in an open class race. The Yamaha challenge to Honda dominance was growing stronger by the day. The RD56 had been revamped since its first appearance at Suzuka in 1961. With no research and development track of their own, the company had been forced to test the machine in its initial stages of production on a 9ft wide path alongside the Tenryū River. Given that the machine was theoretically capable of 135mph it made for the frightening prospect of a high speed dunking for the test rider, if anything were to go wrong.

The two-stroke, forward-inclined engine was a parallel twin, with rotary valves. The layout was fairly conventional, except for the fact that the cooling fin was a little larger and the rotary valves were fitted to the right and left crankshaft ends. It had a maximum output of 45 brake horsepower (bhp) at 11,000rpm. The carburettor was a Mikuni type with a separate float chamber. Yamaha had experienced difficulties early in their Grand Prix career with bubbling petrol, and it was hoped this would overcome these problems. The RA75, the 125cc model, although it was expected at the TT did not make a public appearance until the Japanese Grand Prix, much later in the season. Yamaha still stated that 125cc single-cylinder machines were capable of doing the job. Twin-cylinder machines were not yet part of their thinking for this class.

Once again, the press were out in force to welcome Yamaha to the Isle of Man. The newspaper and television reporters were desperate to discover just what Yamaha had done in their efforts to unseat rivals Honda and Suzuki from the top spot. With the withdrawal of MV Agusta from the smaller classes, as well as that of the East German MZ firm, these would now be a three-cornered fight between the Japanese factory teams. In the 125cc race, Suzuki were dominant, taking a one-two-three with Hugh Anderson, Frank Perris and Ernst Degner. Although Yamaha did not compete in the 50cc event it was also a Suzuki benefit, with the added bonus that Suzuki rider Mitsuo Itoh became the first Japanese competitor to win a TT race. That just left the 250cc Lightweight race as Yamaha's only chance of success, and four of their machines had been entered for it. Fumio Itoh was supported by Yoshikazu Sunako, Hiroshi Hasegawa, as well as Englishman Tony Godfrey, who had been signed up by the team purely for TT duties. He remembered in an interview later:

> I was not the first choice. Percy Tait turned it down. I was given the bike just for the TT. There were no contracts and I was not paid anything. I was a poor businessman and didn't worry too much about cash. I reckoned it was worth the risk just to get a works ride and if I did well I could join the team and then get paid for it. Getting the ride didn't really have anything to do with me. The opportunity came because I was signed with Shell and I think they asked Lew Ellis [the Shell competition manager] if he could recommend any likely runners. After Percy Tait said no, I said yes. To me, it was the chance every rider dreams of. I do remember riding the bike during practice, I could not believe it was a 250. It went past 500 Manx Nortons as if they were going the other way![1]

In practice, Honda's Jim Redman was the quickest, followed by Tommy Robb similarly mounted, but Itoh and Godfrey had placed third and fourth fastest respectively. For Godfrey this was a particularly impressive achievement because of his unfamiliarity with the machine. Godfrey spoke to commentator Murray Walker at the weigh-in the day before the race:

> I think that the position is very much as when Honda first came over. No one took very much notice of them, and yet they proved to be a force to be, what, more than reckoned with, and I feel that, quite honestly, the Yamahas will be the same. They are going extremely well. They are very, very much lighter [than British bikes], but they are doing about the same speed. They jump from bump to bump, and the handling is very, very good. Extremely good. I couldn't tell you how many gears [it has], I just keep pressing until they stop going, you know? I just lose count! We work to between nine and eleven thousand on the revs, normally. I think they'll do the six laps, quite honestly. We've had some trouble with oiling of plugs, but they seem to have cured it, they've had no other type of mechanical trouble whatsoever.[2]

Race day dawned bright and clear, with scorching temperatures soon turning the road surfaces into slippery rivers of melting tar. Many a rider would come to grief that day in what the press dubbed the 'slip and slide' TT. As the flag dropped Honda machines led the field away, followed by the Yamahas behind. The Honda riders had everything to lose, and the Yamaha men everything to gain. By the end of the first lap the sheer power of the Yamaha was obvious for all to see, with a radar trap clocking Godfrey at 140.2mph and Itoh at 138.3mph. The Honda of Redman had been pushed into third place. With a disadvantage in straight line speed, all Redman could fall back on was riding skill, but he had plenty of that. He managed to get ahead of Itoh, whilst Godfrey was forced to stop to make adjustments. Whilst fighting his way back into the race, he slid off when the gearbox seized near Milntown, and was badly injured. Godfrey was the first-ever racer to be airlifted from the roadside to a hospital in the rescue helicopter, and he was to spend ten days unconscious at Ramsey Cottage Hospital. Over the years that followed, he would keep in touch with the matron who had cared for him during that time, and even had a reunion with her in 2007. Itoh meanwhile had retaken the lead, but the race was won and lost in the pits at the half way stage after lap three. His pit stop was twenty-five seconds adrift of Redman's, and it put him out of contention for a win. None the less, Itoh came home in second place, a major achievement for the Yamaha firm. In this, the toughest of all races, they had thrown down a gauntlet to the world. Naito recalled afterwards: 'After the 1963 TT, when Itoh finished second to Jim Redman's Honda, we had a great boost of confidence in our machines.'[3] The significance was not lost on Jim Redman, who commented:

> Boy, those Yamahas were going like hell. I had to pull out all the stops to get some advantage back. We'll have to get some more speed from somewhere. The bike I had was nowhere near as quick. If Yamaha had been fielding a rider with a good knowledge of the TT, I think I might have lost it. But I'm sure they'll soon put that right. They're obviously in the business seriously. And, knowing the Japanese, they'll move heaven and earth to build on what they've got ... and that means getting some real good men.[4]

Later that year, after a test ride in Japan, a new face joined the Yamaha squad. Luton-born Phil Read had first approached

Itoh at the 1963 TT. Never a man to play down his own talent, and spotting an opportunity after his campaign on Gilera machines with Scuderia Duke had fizzled out, Read did not wait to be invited. At 24 years of age the rather abrasive young Englishman demonstrated a fierce will to win, and had already stood on the top step of the podium in the 1961 Junior TT. Allied to this was a burgeoning skill, that was to give him a reputation as a rider who could usually be relied upon to be in the thick of the final action at the chequered flag. He was just the sort of man Yamaha needed – and they were quick to recognize his potential, even if he himself had been the one to first point it out to them.

Having travelled to Japan for testing purposes, Read found much that he admired about the Japanese and their way of working. The factories were efficient, and their workers were motivated and proud of the Yamaha name. They all worked together for the common good, and made best use of their collective resources. In a two-stroke exhaust, controlling the resonance of pressure waves is all-important in obtaining more speed; the resonance can be judged from the pitch of the exhaust note. Yet instead of wasting valuable time in trying to understand this, the motorcycle engineers simply handed the problem to the company's musical instrument division to solve. As Read later ruefully observed, in a British factory at this time, that would probably have caused a strike. He also found that he was on the same page as the Yamaha technicians in constantly seeking more power from the engines. Coming into the pits, and having a team of dedicated mechanics working in an orderly fashion with the objective of getting rider and machine out again as fast as possible was a new experience for Read, who had previously only encountered the disorganisation and internal tensions of Scuderia Duke.

Whatever difficulties would later arise between Phil Read and Yamaha, there can be no doubt that it was he who really put them on the map in the racing world. Signing him marked the turning point in their fortunes; he brought the vital missing ingredient to the table. At this time, the Japanese motorcycle factories needed Western riders in order to aid development. In Japanese culture, it would not be considered polite for a test rider to point out the faults in a prototype. A Japanese employee would sometimes continue riding a machine that he knew was defective, rather than suffer what was seen as the embarrassment of speaking candidly about its faults to his employers. The Western riders carried no such cultural baggage, and were more than happy to tell their employers exactly what was wrong in terms of handling and performance, and how it should be corrected. The Japanese riders had been good competitors, Itoh especially so, but they lacked Read's steely resolve and spark of genius. He was never a man who was particularly well liked by fellow riders – his towering sense of his own ability made sure of that – but what his rivals did have for him was respect, albeit of the grudging variety.

Read came into the team just as the RD56 was finally becoming a machine with World Championship capability. It needed to be paired with a rider as tough and determined as Read (just as Honda had such a man in Jim Redman) and there can be no doubt that he got the best from it. His first outing aboard the RD56 was at Suzuka in the 1963 Japanese Grand Prix. Despite encountering engine problems Read delivered a flawless performance. It was a race run at blistering speed, and he gained the respect both of Redman and of the excited crowd of Yamaha officials, who signed him up for the 1964 season directly after the race. Read's contract was then worth £10,000, about £200,000 in today's terms.

Also for the upcoming 1964 season, Yamaha signed a young Canadian rider, Mike Duff, as a back up for Read. He was to contest the 250cc class at only three events that year, the Isle of Man TT, Dutch TT and Belgian Grand Prix. Ideally, he would have liked a contract for the whole season, but a works ride in any shape or form was not to be sniffed at. Read and Duff were good friends, and the former had some influence with Yamaha in getting him the ride. As Duff recalled later:

> Of the four riders on the short list ... I offered the least threat to his team leadership, but I possessed sufficient ability to be a competitive second runner to back-up his world title efforts. Without question, Read was the faster rider, but in 1964, it remained unanswered how much better I would become in future years. I later learned that I had been Yamaha's fourth choice. Oil company contracts had excluded [Derek] Minter and [John] Hartle, and [Alan] Shepherd wouldn't accept the three-ride contract.[5]

For Duff it was his first experience of riding machinery which he had not prepared himself, but he had no need to worry. The Japanese were nothing if not meticulous and at no time did he ever feel that preparation was anything less than thorough. Yamaha believed that each rider caused patterns of wear on a motorcycle which were as individual to him as a fingerprint. For this reason, they assigned a particular engine mechanic to each rider. It was this man's job to know the engine inside out and to ensure that it was set up and tuned correctly for the man who was to ride it. Duff's mechanic was Kaneyoshi Suzuki (known as Suzuki-san), and a good working relationship developed between them.

Itoh, the veteran, was scheduled mainly for TT duties, as was Tony Godfrey, whilst the other Westerners would also contest the other World Championship rounds. In the event however, neither Godfrey nor Itoh would ride in the Isle of Man that year due to the lingering effects of earlier crashes. Worldwide motorcycle sales had escalated dramatically, and millions of dollars' worth of business were now at stake. The vast sums of money being made by Yamaha were channelled back into racing – the target was the world titles currently held by Honda, and the cost of taking them simply did not matter – money was no object at this time. Redman's all-conquering 250cc Honda might have been more reliable than its Suzuki or Yamaha rivals, but it was demonstrably slower in a straight line than the latter. In Read they had a rider who was almost Redman's equal, and Yamaha now smelled blood in the water.

The RD56 had benefitted from a massive injection of cash into the research and development fund, but its Achilles Heel was still the fact that its two-stroke twin-cylinder engine was air-cooled. Successful cooling of the engine was the Holy Grail in motorcycle racing at this time, and all three of the major Japanese manufacturers were trying to crack it. Yamaha engines were particularly prone to seize if they got too hot, and the consequences could be terrifying. A rider usually had little or no warning, and could be thrown down the road by a locked up engine. Nevertheless, although bore and stroke were unchanged, power had now increased from 40bhp to over 54bhp at 11,000rpm. This was achieved mainly through greater efficiency in the engine – the combustion chamber was semi-spherical; the clearing ports were of an orthodox shape, but port number three was made especially large. The floating rotary valve was lubricated by means of an oil pump, similarly the crankshaft bearing. The Mikuni carburettor had been adapted to prevent fuel from bubbling and causing cut-outs. The parallel twin crankshafts were independent of each other, and each transmitted power through a gear to the idler shaft. Power from the idler shaft was supplied to the Mitsubishi racing magneto above the transmission at the rear of the crank. Rotation was minimised to half turns and the magneto end points formed two crests. The bike had a multi-plate dry clutch and seven gears. The frame was a Kuromori double cradle, essentially unchanged from the previous model. The rear brake had a new unique adjuster, a thumb operated lever on the collar between the left handlebar grip and the clutch lever mounting. This lever was connected by cable to an eccentric on the brake fulcrum, and by pushing the lever forward, any slack detected by the rider at the foot pedal could be taken up.

By the time the teams reached the Isle of Man round of the 1964 World Championship it had become a gruelling slogging match between Honda and Yamaha, but the result was still wide open. There was a real pressure cooker atmosphere that year; the Isle of Man lives and breathes racing during the TT fortnight. For the riders there was no escape from it, and nowhere that they could go and avoid recognition by the thronging TT crowds. Read posted a lap of 96.6mph in practice. He had been using a 1963 model for the early races of that season, but in June at the Isle of Man Yamaha unveiled Read's new 1964 mount for the first time, the updated RD56. He spoke to commentator Murray Walker about how his machine compared with the 1963 version:

> The differences are that its lower, and its slightly longer, its lighter, and there's ten percent more power. But I've yet to take the new Yamaha to a circuit where I've ridden the old Yamaha, to compare it, but it definitely seems a lot better. It's the same engine, with a few modifications that have given the extra power. The frame is different,

but that's about all really, and improved streamlining ... reliability is the $60,000 question, we've been having a lot of trouble in practice with 'pug truggles' as the Japanese say! Its rather difficult. Carburation difficulties have come from finding the correct type of plug for the conditions; too soft a plug and they seize; the next grade of plug, slightly harder and they oil up.[6]

Really however, this undersold what, if looks alone were anything to go by, was one of the most captivating machines ever introduced to a racing public. Aesthetically, it was second to none. Painted mainly in gleaming white, it featured a 6-inch red stripe which ran across the top of the fuel tank and continued across the tip of the seat fairing. This red stripe also ran across the sides of the front fairing and through the oval number plates. The bodywork hugged the outline of the machine, and the seat followed the lines of the fuel tank, and adopted a new square look which would be the signature of Yamaha racing machines in the next decade. Mindful of their defeat through a longer pit stop the previous year, the 1964 RD56 also featured an enormous 8-gallon-tank, which the designers hoped would be sufficient for four laps, and would thus necessitate a shorter refuelling stop. It remained to be seen however if carrying the extra weight at the start of the race would affect handling over the first two laps.

In practice week, Yamaha were cautious in preserving their engines, and also did not wish to give too much away to the ever watchful spies from rival camps. Duff recalled that it was a case of one lap only before the machine was back in the pits for mechanics to pore over the mysteries of spark plug discolouration. Excessive fouling on the plug indicated a fuel and oil mixture that was too rich. A lack of discolouration might indicate that the mixture was too lean, which would mean an increase in engine temperature and consequent expansion of the piston beyond the bore of the cylinder, resulting in sudden and potentially catastrophic seizure. During the Monday morning practice session he surprised himself by going 2mph faster than Read, but still he was limited by the mechanics to one lap. By the third session, on the Tuesday morning, the mechanics allowed him to put in two laps for the first time, meaning that when he passed the start/finish line he would be embarking on his debut flying lap. Duff, who was more used to ponderous and heavy British machines, was still not fully aware of what his powerful little 250cc Yamaha was really capable of. He crested Bray Hill flat out, and half way down grabbed as much brake as he could and worked frantically down through the gears in an effort to scrub off some speed. To say that he approached Quarter Bridge off line would be something of an understatement, and with his heart pounding, he struggled to stay aboard as he swooped through the right-hander.

The 250cc Yamaha had no useable power below 9,000rpm, but at 10,000rpm the acceleration was almost uncontrollable until a maximum of 11,000rpm was reached. Below 9,000rpm plug fouling was also extremely commonplace. To ensure a clean acceleration at the start of a race, the engine would be warmed up using a practice set of plugs, to rid it of excess oil. When it was switched off to await the drop of the flag, the race plugs would then be fitted. When the engine fired at the start of the race it would immediately be accelerated to 11,000rpm, the start being the only time the engine would then be below 9,000rpm. The seven speed gearbox made maintaining high revs relatively straight forward, and it also proved itself to be extremely resilient, the rider on average making a gear change every three seconds during the course of a two hour race.

However the tiny high revving power unit provided almost no engine braking, and this could take some getting used to by a rider who was new to two strokes.

Belfast man Tommy Robb, unceremoniously dumped by Honda, had now joined the Yamaha squad as a replacement for Itoh who had been injured at the Singapore Grand Prix earlier in the season. He had a real point to prove against his former employers. He remembered:

> [the new team] couldn't have been kinder, but the bikes took some sorting out, for they suffered from chronic plug trouble. In fact, in practice I began to despair of ever having a flying lap down Bray Hill, for I usually got no further than Quarter Bridge. Things got really rough on early morning practice when I stopped and ran out of plugs on the Mountain – and believe me there is no lonelier place in the world at that time of the day!
>
> I had used my half dozen plugs and had begun to despair, when I spotted an old tractor in a field. I raced across with my plug spanner, took a rusty plug out of the tractor, put my Yamaha plug in its place, tried the bike; it fired first time, and I was off again. The plug carried me back to the start, much to my relief. So there's a farmer somewhere up there around Ramsey Bay with a flying tractor now![7]

In the 250cc race, held in superb weather on Monday afternoon, Mike Duff was out with engine trouble minutes after the start of the event, coasting to a stop at the Highlander with a holed piston. Read was soon in the pits with plug trouble and lost valuable time. Redman continued his relentless pace, and Robb's Yamaha was the only one of the three factory machines to finish, after also stopping for a plug change. He pushed in from Governor's Bridge to take seventh place behind the Yamaha privateer machine of Roy Boughey. For whatever reason, carburettor jetting was the real weakness of the Yamaha factory engine that year, and it was a particular problem on the Isle of Man. In some places the Mountain Course is close to sea level, where the air is denser and a richer mixture is needed. When the course reaches higher ground less fuel is needed. Keeping the engine in the optimum power band resulted in plugs oiling, but in order to fix this problem Read suggested a handlebar mounted control to enable the rider to adjust the mixture, according to the road conditions. The idea was taken up by the factory, showing the way in which riders and mechanics worked together as a team in those early years.

Yamaha had also brought to the Isle of Man another RD56, bored out to 252cc, for Read to ride in the Junior TT. Although it was reported to be incredibly fast, it was not used. Anything other than the 250cc World Championship campaign was considered by the company at this time to be a distraction, and received secondary attention. However, the following year the firm had more confidence, and would make an attempt at the Junior race.

Towards the end of the 1964 season, Honda had unveiled a new weapon in this ongoing war of attrition. The Honda 3RC164 was – for a time – the biggest secret in racing and was not revealed until the teams reached Monza for the Italian Grand Prix. Yamaha company director Takehiko Hasegawa stated:

We realised that the new Honda Six, unveiled at Monza, was a serious threat to Yamaha for the new season, 1965. It was claimed to produce 60hp and our RD65 was already near to its limit of power, even though the initial 40hp had been increased to 54.5hp. We did not expect its maximum output to be raised to a level of 60hp and we decided on a new machine to replace it – the RD05. We adopted a V-four layout for this machine and wanted to raise the power output to around 70hp. We weren't too interested in a square-four layout which had been unsuccessful with Suzuki's RZ racer – and the rotary disc mechanism did not allow the adoption of an in-line four layout.

Our new development programme started right after the Japanese Grand Prix in October 1964. We had completed the first V-four engine before the opening of the 1965 season and the maximum power output was well in excess of 65hp – with room for improvement and development as the season went on.[8]

However, as things transpired, the new machine would not reach Europe until the closing stages of the 1965 season. Before that year's campaign began, Yamaha had decided to provide full back-up facilities for the team only in the Isle of Man, Holland and Belgium. They would then withdraw the full team, leaving only one mechanic. Before they pulled back to Japan the back-up team comprised Hasegawa, team manager; Masaharu Naito, chief engineer, experiencing his first season in Europe; and a money manager named Watanade. There were also three engineers and five mechanics drawn from the thirty-strong racing department at the Hamamatsu factory.

Read was to be number one in the team, with Duff once more in support. John Cooper, the British rider, had been suggested as a third member of the squad, but this was vetoed by Read who instead favoured the up and coming Bill Ivy. Born in Maidstone, Kent, Ivy was described as one of racing's last great characters. He was small in stature, but made up for it with a flamboyant personality. He had long hair, wore flower-power shirts, and turned up at race meetings in the noisiest of sports cars. Despite his diminutive size he had tremendous upper body strength, and in racing he was utterly fearless. One of his sponsors, Frank Higley wrote to Yamaha asking to buy the best machine that they could sell him for Ivy to ride, money being no object. The Japanese were intrigued by this display of confidence and invited Ivy for a test ride. He did well, and proved Read's point. Accordingly, Ivy was given a temporary contract covering only the Isle of Man and Dutch TTs. Mike Duff for his part was pleased to be back on the Isle of Man once more, remembering:

> The return to the Island was a welcome relief from the hectic weekly treks across Europe. I looked forward to the stop in one place for a two week period and to the TT circuit itself. Even though the short stay would include many sleepless nights and frequent early mornings, I always enjoyed the Isle of Man TT Races. They were a necessary school in discipline. The constant ride against the clock, rather than other riders, the continuous change in corner variations, the demands the course places on memory and personal confidence, hones a rider's timing and riding ability. Through the need for self preservation the course develops consistency. No other racing complex sharpens these necessary traits to such a fine degree in such a short space of time like the 37 ¾ mile Mountain Circuit. To me, the TT was necessary, even considering the cost factor and personal risk.[9]

Bill Ivy was less enamoured of the place, and said so openly. Part of the problem was his lack of familiarity with the Mountain Course, but as a professional rider who had just secured a lucrative works contract, he knew that he was going to have to just knuckle down and get to grips with it.

The first practice session took place in foul weather, but it proved that the carburation refinements offered by the new enrichening jet mechanism which had been developed by Yamaha over the winter really did work. It was now difficult to foul plugs unless revs dropped to an unrealistically low level. Confounding expectations, Ivy took to the more powerful 250cc machinery more quickly than the 125cc model. This was not however to say that he did not have some hair-raising moments. He told reporters:

> I had one particularly nasty moment at the top of Bray Hill. I was going through flat out on the 250 when the rear wheel left the ground on a little bump. The revs soared and when the wheel hit the ground again the front-end reared up. Phew! I shut down after that. Although two-stroke engines have a reputation for seizing, you never think yours is going to, but if it does you just have to be ready. During practice the smaller Yamaha seized at the end of the Sulby Straight, and the 250 at an almost flat-out left hander near Rhencullen. Fortunately. I whipped the clutch in quickly enough on each occasion.[10]

Duff had not minded being second string rider, but it looked now that he might be pushed back to third man, which did not bode well for his future prospects within the team. Read meanwhile laid down the gauntlet in practice with a near 100mph lap on the 250cc machine. It was Yamaha's 125cc bike which really created a sensation however when it was recorded at 126mph through the speed trap at the Highlander, which is not even the fastest part of the course.

Yet in spite of this success, all was not well in the Yamaha camp. Disagreements between Read and Duff over tactics, as well as the latter's misapprehensions regarding the unpredictable handling of the 250cc machine, led to discord. As the dawn of the first race approached, the Lightweight TT on the Monday, a thick white mist enveloped the Island. Strong winds soon blew it away however, leaving only Snaefell mountain topped in white cloud. The Isle of Man had brought Read and Redman together once more to settle old scores. However, Read's towering ambition would prove to be his undoing. Whilst for his masters at Hamamatsu, the true prize was a race win and the World Championship points that this would bring, for Read the glory lay in being the first rider to lap the Mountain Course at over 100mph on a 250cc machine.

On the first circuit, Read obliterated the record from a standing start by lapping at 100.01mph. It was astonishing stuff; by the time Redman completed his first lap he was sixteen seconds down on the Yamaha. This was unprecedented and at first it was assumed to be a timing error. When it was shown to be correct, wiser heads questioned the wisdom of Read's apparent determination to crush the Honda into the dust with his breakneck speed. Then it happened. On the second lap a crankpin broke in his engine, and Read's Yamaha was out. Redman saw it happen, and recounted:

> I planned to stay with [Read], and if he had given me an opportunity I would have gone through, because if you are in front you can do exactly what you want to do, and if you are behind you sometimes have to shut off when you don't want to, and those two strokes, the more they shut off and turn on again, the more likely they are to give trouble. So I tried to keep up with Phil, hoping I'd get a

chance to slip through and maybe slow him up on a slow section and maybe oil a plug for him! He went away from me steadily, and I think he must have had about three seconds' lead when the bike seized. I could see him, we were going up the Mountain Mile at the time, and we got about three quarters of the way up there, and I suddenly saw Phil sit up and grab the clutch and I thought, 'You beauty, she's blown!'[11]

Ivy then moved up to challenge Redman, but by lap four the weather was deteriorating and his unfamiliarity with the course began to tell. Uncertain of exactly where he was, he went off the racing line, and crashed whilst avoiding another rider in the mist on the Mountain. Bravely he remounted and tried to rejoin the race, but the engine was smashed and he was forced to coast back to the pits. Once there, officials carried him to the medical tent for his injured hip to be attended to. His bravery earned him a special place in the hearts of the Yamaha mechanics, who were already admiring his skill and determination as a rider. Mike Duff, the third rider, remembered that by this stage a greasy film of dew had descended on the roads, causing lap times to fall. He was too far adrift to seriously challenge Redman but still made second place. On paper, this ranked as his most successful race on the Island, and he should have been pleased, but Duff could not recall ever feeling more depressed after a race, simply because of the atmosphere within the Yamaha camp.

Read for his part came in for heavy criticism for his lack of caution, which had caused his Yamaha to break under the stress. Following the race, he and Duff had a fierce argument about their relative performances; Duff knew that he had ridden poorly and did not need to be told as much by his team mate. In his defence, he told Read that at least he had managed to finish. Read was not in the least apologetic for his attitude, and was evidently more interested in his own results than that of the team.

The opportunity came to restore some balance, however, with another outing in the 125cc Ultra-Lightweight race at that year's Isle of Man TT. For Duff, practice on the smaller machine had been bedevilled by a persistent misfire. Mechanics suggested that maybe it was caused by the close-fitting fairing which restricted air flow to the carburettors and led the engine to run too rich. The team spent all of Tuesday in race week at Jurby airfield in the north of the Island, trying to iron out this problem. Small holes were cut in the lower part of the fairing near the carburettor intakes, in order to allow more air to reach them. After adjusting the jets, the misfire seemed to be cured. They were late weighing in, but the mechanics were now more confident of success. Phil Read was rather less so, and told Murray Walker:

> Oh it's a terrific little machine, and its quite easy to ride after the 250. It's difficult to tell [how it will do in the race] because I haven't been able to get with the Honda or the Suzuki to compare the speed, but I think they're as fast. I remember at the Japanese Grand Prix last year, the Suzukis had a bit more top end speed, and the Hondas were about the same, if not just a little more, but now Yamaha has improved the 125, and I think they've got a little bit more power still … We haven't managed to get them to run for more than about one lap properly, yet. [We've had] piston trouble, calibration trouble … very technical! Not to sound too pessimistic, but I'm a bit worried about how I'm going to get back down from the Mountain to start the 350 race.[12]

On their debut in 1965, Yamaha's new 125cc twins were to finish first and third in the hands of Read and Duff, and an older air-cooled model took seventh place, ridden by Ivy. This was a first outing for the water-cooled RA97 and the hopes of many at Yamaha were pinned on it as a blueprint for the future. Race day dawned bright and clear, with a warm breeze. In the 1960s it was customary to start a race with a dead engine and push start away from the line with the bike in first gear. To the dismay of the Yamaha racing manager Hasegawa, Mike Duff was still astride his machine when the flag dropped. He shouted at him to dismount and push, but the little Yamaha was so light that it was possible for him to paddle forward with both feet then drop the clutch, the machine duly fired and he accelerated cleanly away, to Hasegawa's great relief. Duff set off just ahead of Suzuki's Hugh Anderson, and had no official plan other than to prevent Anderson from catching him. Half way into lap one however, the New Zealand rider had caught him on the road, but his challenge would not last; his race was effectively ended by a fouled plug.

Because Anderson had caught him so easily, Duff was surprised to see a pit board which showed him in second place, two seconds down on Phil Read. Read however was flying and soon stretched that advantage to eight seconds. Over the Mountain on the last lap, Duff poured in every ounce of effort that he could, trying to catch him. Rushing through Kate's Cottage the little bike was giving all it had, and he had pulled back four seconds on Read at this point. On the charge down to Creg-ny-Baa Duff sat up and braked hard, going down through the gears as he did so. He deliberately ran wide into the pub car park in order to take the right hander with more speed. As he tried to accelerate away, to his dismay he realised that the machine was only firing on one cylinder. Thoughts flashed through his mind; should he stop and change the plug? That would probably cost more time than could be recovered when back running on two cylinders. There were only a few miles left to race, but at Governor's the engine almost gave up completely, yet still he reached the finish line to place third.

Read also lost a cylinder, but it happened so late in the race that it did not materially affect the outcome. He rode his machine superbly to beat the previous year's winner, the Swiss ace Luigi Taveri on a Honda, by six seconds. He showed, at long last, that he did have the necessary qualifications to deliver Yamaha a win the world's most difficult race, and stood on the podium to receive the black and white winner's sash for that first triumph. In contrast with the Lightweight race, Duff was well satisfied with third, and felt that this was one of his best performances. Ivy had averaged over 90mph in a closely fought race, and his top-ten finish was enough to give the Japanese concern the much coveted manufacturer's award.

Read also competed in the Junior TT on an over-bored 254cc Yamaha machine later that day. He was giving away nearly 100cc in terms of capacity to his Honda and MV rivals, but in conversation with Murray Walker, Read refused to rule his machine out of contention:

> I think they've just got the edge on speed, and probably they handle just as well, so I should think I'll be down a bit on speed ... I think the fastest lap in the 350 is 101, well MVs are having trouble with the handling of their three-cylinder, and Jim [Redman] I think will be scratching to get round at much more than that, and I think it is quite possible for the Yamaha to do 101.[13]

In the event Mike Hailwood, a hot favourite with his MV Agusta, was forced to retire with an oil leak; Read diced for much of the distance with Giacomo Agostini, who was making his TT debut that year, and pushed him into third place, finishing second behind Honda's Jim Redman.

Yamaha clearly still had development work to do; reliability over a long race was not guaranteed, and the braking system had room for improvement, but overall they had much to be pleased about. New machines were on the way from Japan to be tested in England – new air-cooled and water cooled four-cylinder 250cc machines among them. Phil Read held on to the 250cc World Championship, and Duff achieved second place in the final standings, though the end of the year brought new concerns for Yamaha. The firm was still experiencing teething troubles with the V-four engines, but in testing at Suzuka in Japan late in the year Mike Duff was seriously injured. His would be a long and painful road to recovery, although he did eventually ride for the company again. Ominously, rumours were also swirling around the paddock and in the motorcycle press that Mike Hailwood, the greatest rider of his generation, had fallen out with MV Agusta and was now in negotiations to ride in 1966 for Yamaha's biggest rival – Honda. With their number two rider now out of contention for the foreseeable future, Yamaha executives made an urgent long distance phone call to Maidstone in Kent. Mrs Ivy answered the telephone – to learn that her son Bill was back in the team.

Chapter Two

1966–1968
WHO WEARS THE CROWN?

For the 1966 season, Yamaha put forward their best possible pairing – Phil Read, the previous year's 250cc world champion, and Bill Ivy, who was now given a full-time contract. With water-cooled equipment to now draw upon, their chances looked distinctly promising. However, handling was still a problem, tending to negate the efforts the engineers had made to consolidate stamina and maintain performance. Yamaha began the season with the air-cooled 250cc twin and later switched to the water-cooled V-four, but the new model was still bedevilled by handling problems and big-end breakages. The 1966 TT was unusual in that it was affected by the National Union of Seaman's strike that year. Because of the near impossibility of getting teams and fans to the Island it was postponed until August, by which time some of the World Championship titles had already been decided. By this point in the year some manufacturers would usually withdraw from a particular class, if they were no longer in contention, but the 1966 TT still attracted a near record entry. All of the major manufacturers said that they would support it, as a win in the Island was considered to be important in its own right regardless of World Championship standings.

Bill Ivy had been badly injured in the Hutchinson 100 race at Brands Hatch some weeks earlier, and was still not fully fit. He arrived at his usual guesthouse, Mrs Lee's in Douglas and tried to get as much rest as possible. He was however still troubled by violent headaches and bouts of blurred double vision. Despite this, he was determined not to let Yamaha down. His old school motto was 'Service and Courage' and this was the code by which he had tried to live his life. He did not want to let down the team which had been so good to him. The Japanese had given him his big break, they had paid him well, and they had accepted him not only as a rider but as a friend. Ivy-san was conscious of his duty towards them, and was not going to fail them. He made up his mind that he was going to ride.

There was just one drawback. Race officials would not allow him to practice for the first two days, and then they insisted that he should obtain a medical certificate showing that he was fit to ride before allowing him on to the course. So Ivy went to see a local doctor and asked him to look at his back, still scarred and bruised from the Brands Hatch accident. The doctor asked if it hurt, to which he replied a little but not badly enough to prevent him riding. The subject of his concussion never came up, so Ivy walked out of the surgery with the necessary certificate and somehow struggled through practice week.

Mike Duff, battling to regain form after his crash the previous year, was also back on the Island again – his ambition which had driven him on in his darkest moments of despair while in his hospital bed was finally achieved – but he was effectively now a Yamaha satellite rider. The factory would not issue him with a full works contract until he proved his ability once more, but he had access to factory machinery, and entered an ex-works motorcycle as a privateer. The arrangement had its downside – he had to do most of his own maintenance, and learn how to strip and rebuild the engine as well as set up his own carburation, but also had its upside: he did not feel the constant pressure to go faster which came from being part of the official team. During practice week he had put in some good times until a broken main bearing inside the engine caused it to seize abruptly, during the Thursday afternoon practice session, at Sulby Bridge. With lightening reactions he had pulled the clutch as soon as it occurred and the machine came slithering to a halt. He managed to rebuild it in time for Monday's 250cc race, but suffered problems on the start line when it initially refused to fire up. Having changed the plugs in front of the Grandstand he eventually set off, six minutes behind, but the engine failed again on lap two. Overall the 1966 250cc Lightweight TT was a disaster for Yamaha. All of their machines suffered mechanical problems, and none finished. Ivy however put in a lap over the magic 100mph before retiring on the fourth lap, whilst battling for second place. Through the speed trap his machine had been clocked at 150.6mph, and only Hailwood and Agostini would better this during the whole of race week – both of them whilst mounted on 500cc machines.

In practice for the 1966 125cc Ultra-Lightweight TT, Yamaha had tested a new four-cylinder machine, but decided not to race it. Bill Ivy told commentator Murray Walker: 'Well, it's a long race, and we're going to give it a little bit more time to develop. The handling is a little better in the four, but we know that the twin is good. Its reliable.'[1]

The biggest challenge was to come from the Honda five, and Suzuki twin, and he continued by comparing these to the Yamaha machine:

There is very little difference, the Honda really handles well, ours moves around. They're both reliable ... I'm sure it will last the three laps. Hugh [Anderson] really knows his way around here, he's gone quick in training, so he'll be on his way for sure. He's away first, so he'll have nobody in front of him, and of course, Mike [Hailwood] will be on his way. As usual!²

Phil Read described the improvements that had occurred to the twin since the previous year: 'Its difficult to see that anything has been done, but I think the engine's been made more reliable, and a little faster, apart from that nothing.'³

Unexpectedly, Duff was now offered the chance to ride one of the full factory 125cc twins in the race, as the Yamaha manager wanted to field a team of three. Naturally he accepted, and things looked promising for him when he posted the fourth fastest time on the machine in practice. The 125cc Ultra-Lightweight race on the Wednesday was delayed by drizzle and stubborn mist which hung around for most of the morning. Three times the start was delayed as the organisers waited for an improvement in the weather. On each occasion that the new start time was announced, the diligent Yamaha mechanics consulted their meteorological equipment and made adjustments to their carburation settings accordingly. By 1.30pm when the warm up claxon sounded, the sun was breaking through and the shirt sleeves of the crowd reflected the fact that humidity had dropped and it was noticeably warmer. Yamaha had done their homework; Honda had not. Their mechanics had lounged indolently around their pits, confident that their carburation settings from earlier in the morning would suffice.

As a result, in the event itself carburation problems seriously hampered Mike Hailwood's efforts on the Honda five, but he was still the best placed of the team at the end of lap one, in sixth position. The Honda machines had been set up for cool and damp conditions but with the start delayed, the race was actually run in weather that was warm and dry. All the team's riders experienced difficulties with over-jetting as a result. Luigi Taveri had caused further problems for himself at Ballacraine by running off the track, costing him valuable seconds, whilst Yamaha's Bill Ivy was having the race of his life. Team mate and arch rival Phil Read had been the early race leader but Ivy overhauled him – not through any benevolence from Read however, as Ivy posted a lap of 98.55mph, a phenomenal speed for a 125cc machine. He remembered later:

> When I started in the race I still must have been concussed, otherwise I'd never have gone so fast. It was sheer luck that I didn't crash! On the first lap I'd just managed to catch and pass Taveri when I clouted the straw bales coming out of Schoolhouse Bend at Ramsey. Then I got on to the loose surface at the Gooseneck and clanged against an advertisement hoarding on the bank. Luigi went by as I was sorting myself out. He had a smile all over his face and that annoyed me. I caught him up again on the Mountain Mile. The second lap was a series of slides. The third was enjoyable. Things were back in focus again. No slides, no trouble, and just as fast – lovely.[4]

Mike Duff on the other official works Yamaha meanwhile was in fourth place. He was to hold this position for the entire duration of the event, and he would finish a full minute inside the old race record. Taveri's problems continued and at the end of lap two he pulled into the pits. The mechanics literally turned the machine upside down in an attempt to cure its ailments. He spent over two minutes in the pit lane whilst two of the plugs were changed, and then the machine had to be tilted on to its back wheel to clear the flooded combustion chambers. Both he and Ralph Bryans continued to have carburation problems and

Hailwood passed them both on the road, despite shaking his head in despair at his mechanics to indicate that all was not well with his own mount. The race gave Yamaha a memorable one-two as Ivy came home in first place followed by Read in second. Mike Duff's fourth place gave them the cherished team prize as well. It was Ivy's first TT win, and he broke the previous year's lap record by 1.5mph, setting a new target of 98.55mph. Hailwood's sixth place was Honda's best finish, whilst team mate Luigi Taveri finished in eighth place, and remembered of this race:

> Honda decided to also put Mike Hailwood on the 125. But none of our machines ran properly. In practice, Bill Ivy (Yamaha) had given nothing away and always kept his true form hidden. He started the race twenty seconds behind. When he overtook me, I wanted to follow him. I had to look twice as he almost accidentally crashed. He had stretched his arms and legs out from himself, and it is a mystery to me how he always stayed on the machine and on the track. I was afraid for him and feared the worst. But finally the winner was still named as Bill Ivy. Hailwood finished fifth as the best Honda rider. This race was discussed for a long time. Ivy later told me: 'If I think about what I did back then, I still get goose bumps.' Bill was a step closer to the World Championship ranking.[5]

Afterwards, Ivy caught sight of a film of the race. It was then that he realised just how lucky he had been; when he watched himself taking outrageous risks and bouncing off a wall he frightened himself almost to death. Yet Ivy's success had shown just what sort of courage was necessary to be successful at this level, and he would finish runner up in the 125cc World

Championship, amazingly at his first attempt. Mike Duff, despite a creditable performance on the Isle of Man, knew in his heart that he had not done enough to dislodge Read and Ivy as the team's top riders. Despite indications at the beginning of the year that if his form returned, he might well be offered a works contract once more, at the end of the 1966 season he crated up his Yamaha and returned it to Japan. His letters to the company offering to ride once again as a privateer in the coming season fell on stony ground, and he knew that he would no longer feature in their plans as even a semi-works rider.

For the 1967 season, Honda withdrew from the 50cc and 125cc classes in the World Championships. The latter would now become a straight fight between Yamaha and the Suzukis of Stuart Graham, Yoshimo Katayama and Hans George Anscheidt. In the 250cc class, it would become a slogging match between the Honda sixes of Hailwood and Bryans, and the Yamaha fours of Read and Ivy. Now in its second full year, the 250cc RDO5A had been much improved and it was lighter, lower and more powerful; developing 68bhp at 14,000rpm, it weighed 130kg and was capable of over 150mph. By the end of the season another 2bhp had been squeezed out of the motor by Yamaha engineers. The steering head and rear fork pivot had been strengthened; the former now adjustable and two steering dampers (a normal hydraulic unit plus a vane-type) were fitted, all to improve handling. This followed advice from Reynolds frame expert Ken Sprayson and a long test session with Read and Ivy during the winter. Bore and stroke was 44 x 40.5mm respectively. The power band was very narrow being between 12,000 and 14,000rpm and the gearbox was fitted with eight gears to help keep it on the boil.

In 1967 the Isle of Man TT races celebrated their Diamond Jubilee – it was sixty years since the first pioneer riders set off on the Island's dusty roads. Much had changed since then, and now far from being the pursuit of a few enthusiastic amateurs, the races were the crucible of international industrial rivalry. Monday of race week saw the 250cc Lightweight race. The favourite to win was Mike Hailwood, then on a tally of nine TT victories – one more would see him equal the score of the great Stanley Woods, up to then the most successful TT rider. Ralph Bryans with his Honda six and Derek Woodman of MZ led the field away. They were followed by Motohashi of Yamaha. Bill Ivy set off alongside Bill Smith aboard a Kawasaki, with the last of the Yamaha squad, Phil Read setting off on his own. Among the Yamaha mounted privateers were Bob Farmer and Mike Chatterton. At the end of lap one, Hailwood was leading. He was first on the road through Cronk-y-Voddy, followed by Bill Ivy, Phil Read and Ralph Bryans. At half distance Ivy was twenty-five seconds down on Read when his Yamaha went off song, and then broke a crankshaft. Hailwood won, in spite of handling problems, and told reporters afterwards that Phil Read, who finished second, was an ever present threat. Phil Read for his part told reporters that his Yamaha had been jumping out of gear on occasions and the engine had lost a cylinder several times. Showing his hands covered with blisters, Phil said that even though it was fitted with two steering dampers, the bike still needed a lot of holding. The rider could not relax as he was able to on a Norton, he had to hang on all the time. He also had a couple of heart stopping moments when his Yamaha slid sideways on wet tar.

The 1967 Ultra-Lightweight TT on the Wednesday of race week was won by Phil Read, who told reporters afterwards:

> The first lap was quite steady, I saw that Bill Ivy had gone out, and I thought well, our machines must be faster down

the straights, and I had a reasonably not-too-hectic first lap. I had a bad start, but that's just one of those things, then I got a signal at the start of the second lap that I was minus one second I think, and I couldn't believe this, and I thought well, we must get our finger out a bit. So I went a bit quicker and I saw a signal at the end of the second lap that I was minus four seconds, and I couldn't believe this, and I thought well Stuart [Graham] really must be on his way! I'll have to ride like a maniac in the last lap, just to beat him. He's a fantastic rider, Stuart.[6]

It was Read's second 125cc TT win, but for Bill Ivy there was nothing to celebrate; he had retired on the second lap again with engine trouble. Indeed, the most memorable episode of the entire 1967 TT for him was managing to crash his Ferrari into a wall at Greeba at 140mph, whilst showing off with Mike Hailwood and a barmaid from the Hawaiian Bar. He told the Manx police afterwards that he got a flat tyre going into the corner. Although they couldn't prove otherwise, Ivy was still fined £12 for dangerous driving. Yet his form – and the machine's reliability – improved so much in the later races of the season that he went on to take the 125cc world title.

By the end of 1967, just a year after being flown to Japan and invited to sign a full-time contract, Bill Ivy, the flamboyant little character with an apparently limitless taste for steak and chips (even in the grandest gourmet restaurant) gave Yamaha the return for their money they so keenly wanted. No one, not even Yamaha, could have expected Ivy to do so well in just his second full season. It is fair to say that Ivy was a unique character, a seemingly carefree man who, on the outside, appeared to worry about very little. In fact his sometimes reckless riding style, his hippy style of dress and his love of flashy, noisy American and Italian sports cars, belied his sense of responsibility. In that respect he was very much like his great Honda rival, Mike Hailwood. Off the track, they were inseparable and, indeed, Ivy was much closer to Hailwood than to his own team captain, Phil Read. Outsiders seeing Ivy and Hailwood chatting and laughing and generally enjoying life to the full, with Read somewhat in the background, would have believed that the Yamaha team captain was a man alone. This was true in many ways, for Ivy spent more time night-clubbing and mischief-making with Hailwood than he did in the rather more serious atmosphere of Read's company. A lot that was good about Hailwood rubbed off on his little companion. He learned much from the man he considered to be the absolute maestro of racing, and cared little for Read's views. However, no matter how strong their friendship was off the track, when it came to racing there could be no doubt that Hailwood put Ivy in precisely the same category as Read, that of a rival, a man to be beaten.

It was a different matter altogether for Read in the 250cc World Championship class. This was by far the hardest class to win. In fact, in the history of racing, and even after those hard-fought days of the mid-1960s there was never a more hotly contested title. By the end of the season, he was level pegged with Hailwood at the top of the points list; each man with the same number. It was a difficult situation for the FIM, the sport's controlling organisation. Initially, the governing body said that Read was world champion until it was pointed out that Hailwood had scored more wins, so they reversed their decision, but the FIM steward, Otto Sensberg stated that the matter would not be resolved finally until the FIM Congress in October. Phil Read still hoped that the decision would go his way. He did not have to wait long to find out, and it was bad news because the following day the secretary of the FIM's sporting committee told *Motor Cycle News*, by telephone, that Hailwood was world champion. The confusion arose because the rules had been updated in 1964, but they were only printed in French, and an English translation was only to be published during the week following the 1967 Japanese GP! In the obsolete rules, which were still in circulation in English, the next best score would count in the event of a tie, in which case Phil's fourth second place would hand him the title. The latest version of the rules had it that the number of wins would be taken into account if the seven best scores were equal. It was all rather unsatisfactory and arbitrary; an examination of the scores reveals that Read was much more consistent, with four wins and four-second places, compared to Hailwood's five wins, one second and two thirds. Numbers of people thought that Phil had been robbed of the title, and there was a rash of letters in the British motorcycle press supporting him. One in particular came from a Mr M.P. Firth of Huddersfield. In it he demonstrated how farcical the rules for a tie were. He pointed out that if Hailwood had five wins and two thirds, he would not have won the title, even though he still had more wins than Read, so a second place gave him the title but was not good enough to give Read the crown.

Yet Phil admitted in his autobiography that his form was off in 1967, mainly because his marriage was on the rocks, and his marine business in Guernsey was also failing largely due to the fact that he did not have the time to spend on it. For him marriage was a key ingredient in successful racing, and he missed the support his wife gave him in the early Yamaha years. Having set up a home in Guernsey and started a family, his wife then stayed at home to raise the children. She formed her own circle of local friends. Phil was away for long periods, and when he came back home he found that the house was full of people he did not know. He and his wife had drifted apart. Third came Ivy, making it a year of great personal satisfaction for him. The manufacturers' awards were split between Honda, who took the 250cc title, and Yamaha who were awarded the 125cc honours.

The even greater controversy which surrounded the 1968 season has since become legendary. The year started off with press speculation that it was Ivy, and not Read, who was to be Yamaha's number one rider that year. It turned out to be not far short of the truth. When the strategy for the 1968 campaign was being thrashed out, Ivy was told to bid for the two World Championships titles that most interested Yamaha – the 125 and the 250cc. He already held the 125cc title, but the 250cc crown, once held by Read, was now in the hands of Hailwood and Honda. These team orders formed one of the main reasons for a prolonged dispute between Yamaha's two top riders: having already won a world 250cc title, Read apparently wanted to win the 125cc Championship as well. In fact, their dispute became so well publicised that Yamaha's president, Kawakami, instructed his team manager directly to get it sorted out. Angry telex messages and cables came from the president's office in Japan, underlining the need to get the two men to settle their differences – the company could not afford to have personal squabbles aired so publicly. It was also embarrassing for those such as journalists to have to listen to each criticise the other – the rift was obvious, even after Kawakami's intervention.

The hierarchy at Yamaha in Japan felt that Ivy was consistently faster than Read, that he had the greater potential and, because he was younger, he was a better prospect in the longer term. The fact that Read was beginning to prove himself to be one of the world's finest tacticians did nothing to sway Yamaha's plans.

For, in addition to these practical matters, there was a strong personal relationship between Ivy and the Japanese. They held him in high regard and felt a great deal of affection for him. Contrary to widely held belief, the Japanese are sensitive in this way and tend to behave accordingly. Perhaps it was because they could more easily identify with Ivy; he was open, candid and good at describing the problems associated with the setting up of the machines. More than that, he was clearly incredibly brave.

Read was a rather more reserved, diffident sort of figure than the outgoing Ivy. He objected strenuously to the idea that he should play understudy to Ivy's star role. An ambitious man, with a fierce drive which never left him throughout his racing career and, indeed, in his business life, Read wanted to take the two titles for himself. He thus decided to defy team orders. He felt that he had some justification in this; he had helped Yamaha through their roughest patch and had given his best, and he now wanted whatever glory was going as things were getting a little less difficult.

The hunger to become world champion never left Read. He enjoyed the material benefits that it brought, and the fame that came with it. He told anyone who would listen – knowing full well that it would get back to Ivy – that if the other man wanted to be world champion then he would have to fight for it. A gauntlet had been thrown down and Ivy was happy to pick it up, though it would be no mean feat overcoming a rider of Read's skill and resolve. The animosity and rivalry between the two men had turned into open dislike.

The public nature of this internal disagreement caused the displeasure of the FIM. The sport's governing body did not like the idea that riders should be allowing team mates to win or place higher according to instructions from their parent company, and they liked the idea of the paying public finding out about the existence of these secret orders even less. Read's wrath at Yamaha's decision drove him to a perhaps rather surprising course of action – he had written to the FIM, pointing out what was going on. The sport's controlling body acted quickly. They criticised Yamaha for doing what everybody else with works teams was doing, and upbraided them for their tactics. What happened afterwards is not so clear. It would seem that Ivy now wrote to Yamaha and suggested that the plan be changed; he would be happy with the 250cc title and Read should be allowed to contest the 125cc crown unchallenged. Yamaha back tracked and granted Read the support to challenge for the 125cc title while Ivy went for the 250cc championship. The two riders seemed to have come to an unwritten gentleman's agreement that this was the course of action that they would now take. Yet by the end of the season, after a great deal of bickering between the two men, Read had won both of the titles that had been earmarked for his colleague Ivy.

Read was determinedly single-minded in a way that suggests he never made a decision without having first considered every angle. He was always prepared to make a stand on an issue with which he felt strongly – whether it be safety or money. His lack of enthusiasm in following orders that seemed to do little or nothing to help him achieve his personal ambitions had got him into trouble once before – at the Isle of Man TT, when his bid to be the first man to break the 100mph barrier for 250cc ended with a blown engine. Whatever disenchantment Yamaha felt for him probably stemmed from this rather fraught period of their partnership – even though in the end the product of the disagreement was to be a magnificently achieved double World Championship for Yamaha. Not forgetting, of course, also for Read.

In 1968 however Yamaha faced much less of a challenge than in previous years. Honda, alarmed by the rising cost of Grand Prix racing and feeling that they had achieved just about everything they had set out to do on two wheels, withdrew to focus on developing a racing car for Formula 1 competition. Mike Hailwood, Ralph Bryans and Jim Redman were no longer in contention. In the case of Hailwood, he had been paid a handsome retainer by Honda not to ride for any of their rivals. Suzuki likewise had dropped out, leaving Yamaha as the only Japanese works team. They were so far ahead of their remaining rivals that World Championship success that year seemed to be a foregone conclusion.

It was at the TT races that the antagonism between the two Yamaha riders first began to show itself. Read told Ivy that he was not going to hang around and wait for him in the 250cc race on the Monday. Ivy for his part shrugged his shoulders and did not respond; it seems that he was concerned that if an open argument broke out, the real victim would be Naito, the team manager, who might get in to trouble with the Yamaha chiefs in Japan. In the paddock, Read spoke to journalists about his chances in the event; he was asked what sort of power the Yamaha machine was now achieving:

> There have been figures mentioned of over seventy brake horsepower, I can quite believe this too, the power is really violent, you know? You've got to be careful with the throttle, especially if its wet, too. The frame has been stiffened, and one of the important things we found was the steering head angle, and the top yoke distance between the forks and the steering head, which has made the machine now more easy to control from say, bank to bank. It more easily flicks from right to left.[7]

Both Read and Ivy denied that there were any team orders in place, for the TT at any rate, and both indicated to reporters that they would be riding to win. Read was certain that Mike Hailwood's lap record in this class would fall during the upcoming race, indeed he indicated that he would be disappointed if it didn't, because both he and Ivy had the pace to do it (even if Ivy, being somewhat lighter, would probably have a hairier ride). Also interviewed at the same time was a young, up and coming Yamaha rider, named Rodney Gould. In fact, his machine was a Yamaha-Bultaco special, as he explained:

> Well, I spent the winter in the States, in California, and I had the chance of the Yamaha engine, and we managed to obtain a complete water cooled Bultaco, less engine and radiator, and Ron the mechanic had a pair of Yamaha crank cases and he proceeded to work out the weight distribution and so on and so forth, and by the time I got back to England, the frame was virtually completed. We had a little bit of tidying up to do. I think that winter in the States was of great benefit to my career, it made it a lot easier to come back [to UK racing]. In the 250 race I would like to finish around fourth.[8]

Before the start of the race, Read tried some 'gamesmanship' to try to put Ivy off; during practice he had tried out new wider Dunlop tyres, but declared them to be inferior to the old ones. Now with minutes to go, he demanded that the mechanics put the wider Dunlops on. There was confusion, and even the mild mannered Naito lost his temper. In all probability the tyres were no better, but he was trying to demoralise Ivy by making him think they were superior, and he had an advantage. However, Read's attempt at psychological warfare backfired, for he stung

Ivy into riding as hard as he could. On a day of perfect weather conditions for racing, he was in stupendous form. Ivy shattered Mike Hailwood's lap record set on the Honda six from a standing start, with a blistering opening speed of 105.51mph. This was all the more remarkable considering that speed trap times showed that his machine was down on overall power compared to the previous season. It gave him a fourteen second lead over teammate Phil Read, who lost further time on his pit stop at the end of lap two, but after the fantastic opening lap one of Ivy's exhaust expansion chambers broke off, and he lost power, the engine going down to three cylinders. This put Read into the lead and he had almost half a minute in hand on the fourth lap. Then catastrophically he sustained a puncture in the rear tyre and slithered to a halt back at the pits. At the same time, Ivy who was having to continually change gear to compensate for his misfiring engine, got his foot caught under the gear shift while swooping through the bumpy Milntown section. It tore his boot, gashed his foot and wrenched his ankle back, but even though he believed he had broken his toes he dismissed the idea of retiring and carried on, not seeking medical attention until after the race. He was unaware that he had broken the lap record until after it was all over, telling reporters: 'Frightening isn't it! I didn't realise I was going so fast, and I didn't set out to break it. I was trying to catch Phil.'[9]

It was Yamaha's first 250cc Lightweight TT victory, but they only just achieved it; after the race, winner Ivy had to be lifted off his machine and practically carried to the winner's rostrum, his right foot battered and bleeding. He had just achieved one of the most dramatic 250cc victories ever. Read offered his own version of events as an explanation of what had just happened, in an apparent contradiction of what he had said before the race: 'I did not go so fast because we were riding to team orders and Bill was to win. The rear tyre seemed to have been going down for some time because the handling got progressively worse.'[10] With Read out of contention, Gould brought in the fastest of the non-works Yamahas, finishing in fifth place.

In practice for the Ultra-Lightweight race, Ivy had already demonstrated that he had an advantage over Read due to his smaller stature; on one occasion the two had proceeded together up the Mountain Mile almost wheel to wheel; about half way up, Ivy decided to pull away and Read admitted that there was absolutely nothing he could do about it. Ivy quickly put 50 yards or more of distance between them. Ivy himself was confident that if conditions were right on the day, not only could the 100mph lap barrier be broken but also a race average of over 100mph might be possible.

On the Friday morning came the 125cc Ultra-Lightweight race. With it came more psychological warfare in the Yamaha camp; Ivy fully intended to follow team orders and allow Read to win, but he had no intention of doing it until the very end. Again, Ivy was fast from the outset, setting a second lap speed of 100.32mph and making him the first man to lap the Isle of Man over the 'ton' in this class. Amazingly, this 125cc lap record would stand until 1989, by which time the course had been made much smoother and many bends straightened out. Read was riding desperately, trying to catch him, but Ivy simply turned up the flame. One spectator at the bottom of Barregarrow reported that Ivy came down the hill, standing on the footrests as he fought for control of the machine which had got itself into a terrifying 'tank slapper'. Yet Ivy did not shut off at all, and continued fighting for control at 130mph. At one point the Yamaha mechanics became worried that Ivy was going to go flat out for victory, and one was sent up to Governor's Bridge with a pit board and a stop watch, to make him wait in the dip, if corrected time showed that he was in the lead. They need not have worried. Read duly took victory, when Ivy deliberately slowed on the last lap. In an incredible scene he halted his Yamaha in front of a group of astonished spectators at Creg-ny-Baa, and looking back up the road asked them sardonically where Read was. When he was sure that the watching crowd realised that he was willingly abandoning the crushing superiority that he had established, he set off again and allowed Read to take race victory. Read for his part just missed the 100mph milestone, and had to be content with a new record race average of 99.12mph. He said afterwards, 'I thought I might have done it, but the bikes were slower than in practice because they had been deliberately jetted up to make them more reliable.'[11]

Questioned about conditions out on the road, and whether melting tar had been a problem under the hot sun, he added: 'It's not so bad, really, but you just don't know, you've just got to be careful say at Creg ny Baa, Signpost and Schoolhouse Corner at Ramsey. It does look a bit wet. I wouldn't say it was uneventful, it was leaping around a bit.'[12]

The press were now onto the story and wanted to know if Bill had thrown the race or not. He denied that he had, and claimed that his engine had gone off on the last lap, but his denials were accompanied by a cheeky grin which gave the game away. It was Read's third Ultra-Lightweight victory for Yamaha in four years, and his fourth TT win over all. Unfortunately, for the spectators around the Island it was not a particularly great race as the two Yamahas tore away from the rest of the field, and Read finished almost ten minutes ahead of the third placed rider. It was he who took the ultimate accolade that year, with two world titles to his name; his third 250cc World Championship, and his first at 125cc. Yet it was also to bring the curtain down on his association with the Yamaha factory. They could be ruthless when they needed to be, and as a result of the squabbling Read had now fallen from favour in the eyes of the company hierarchy, but equally well he had seen the writing on the wall – with no new machines in development it was becoming increasingly obvious that the factory was going to withdraw from Grand Prix racing at the end of 1968, and he was going to be out of a job in 1969 in any event, so what was the point in riding to team orders. Read would never ride for Yamaha – officially – again. Ivy for his part was so disgusted with what had gone on in the 1968 season that he vowed to quit motorcycle racing altogether, and planned to take up Formula 2 car racing instead. However, he needed money to get started in that field, and it was for a large pay cheque that he returned to motorcycles temporarily in 1969. It was whilst practising in the East German Grand Prix that year that he was tragically killed; the accident occurred in the Sachsenring outfield away from the view of spectators, so the exact circumstances were never established, but it appeared that whilst he was warming it up his Jawa machine had suffered an engine seizure, and despite all he had learned during his Yamaha years, his hand was not on the clutch, and he was thrown from it. His helmet had not yet been fastened, and came off his head resulting in fatal injuries. The Japanese are sometimes accused of a lack of emotion, but all in the Yamaha hierarchy, particularly the mechanics who had worked with him, were utterly grief stricken by the death of 'Little Bill'.

After Ivy was killed, Yamaha presented his mother with a miniature golden temple, inscribed with the words, 'Bill Ivy – you will always be a winner, on the circuits as well as in our hearts'. They also presented Mrs Ivy with a 350cc racing motorcycle; she might have been forgiven for rejecting it and the sport which had taken the life of her only son, but instead of selling the machine as many people expected, Mrs Ivy chose to involve herself in the world in which her son had been so famous and admired. She got permission from the factory in Japan to enter the bike at race meetings as an Ivy-Yamaha, and she set about with help from others in the sport to find an up and coming rider to campaign it. Through this she encouraged and supported a number of younger competitors. Mrs Ivy also became a sponsor – believed to be the only woman to do so in Europe at this time – and founded a series of challenge races in memory of her son.

It had taken Yamaha eight years to develop their machines to the point where they were equal to – indeed in many ways superior to – those of Honda and Suzuki, who had started before them. However the regulation changes which were now being proposed by the FIM for the forthcoming 1969 and 1970 seasons appeared to many to be aimed squarely at removing the advantage of the technologically superior Japanese factories, by limiting cylinder numbers, gears and overall weight. In dismay, Yamaha also announced that they would withdraw their factory team from Grand Prix competition as a result. The move led in the coming years to the development of local importer supported teams, but more especially it opened the door to privateers, once the stranglehold of the factory teams on World Championship level competition had been broken. For Yamaha perhaps more than any other manufacturer, the TT races of the 1970s would become a spectacular showcase for their machinery and technology.

Chapter Three

1969–1973
THE AGE OF THE PRIVATEER

More so than any other of the major Japanese factories, Yamaha through the 1960s had been developing over-the-counter production racing machines, in parallel with equipment for their own factory team; it was clear to them that there was a huge market among those in racing who wanted top quality factory machinery, but who were operating on a limited budget. As early as 1963, the 250cc TD1 model, based on the YDS-2 street machine, had been offered for sale to the growing privateer market and was a great commercial success, retailing at about £500. It had the same frame and crank case as the street bike, and though it was marketed with lights these were the first things to be removed in privateer hands. The two-stroke parallel twin engine was also lightened by use of a special cylinder, cylinder head and expansion chamber, which took the overall weight down to 95.5kg. A new carburettor with separate float chamber completed the conversion. It now gave an impressive 35bhp at 9,500rpm.

Similarly they developed the 255cc TE1 model, and the export-only TD1-B followed in 1966. It had a 246cc engine and also produced 35bhp, at 10,000rpm, but possessed much greater durability than its fore-runner. Later Yamaha released an even further improved model which could produce 36bhp. On this machine the clutch was relocated to reduce wear and tear and to cure possible oil seal problems; the engine also had five ports to overcome the issue of residual gases impeding combustion. With fuel now entering the combustion chamber through four entry points and exhaust cleared completely, the engine produced more power over a greater spread.

Yamaha's next offering was the TD2 with a claimed 44bhp. The frame was made of high tension steel tube and was of similar design to the RD56, which had a proven history of race success. Ceriani front forks and a high strength box section swing arm completed the picture. In January 1971 came the TDB2 model, incorporating upper and lower crank case sections, again with five ports. Customer demand for a 350cc model resulted in the TR2 model which was based on the road-going R3. The piston valve twin-cylinder engine produced 54bhp. It was equipped with the auto-lube system and also featured Ceriani forks. Although they sold 250 and 350cc production racing machines, Yamaha at first held back on producing a 125cc model. This was despite the fact that they had all the basic ingredients in their AS2, the machine that was the basis of their factory racing machine. Eventually they released the YZ623 which complied with the post 1968 FIM regulations – it was air-cooled with a six-speed gearbox and weighed only 75kg. They also released a water-cooled version, the YZ623A, and both types utilised the 'diamond' frame with a thick single spar backbone, rather than the double cradle type (based on Norton's Featherbed frame) which their other models made use of.

However, more so than with any other type of factory machine, as the 1970s progressed innovative engineers like Britain's Colin Seeley and Frenchman Éric Offenstadt (known by all as Pépé) would take basic Yamaha machines and remodel them, introducing better, stronger frames which were especially suited to bumpy road circuits like that at the Isle of Man TT. Seeley had begun his career as a sidecar racer, whilst Offenstadt had mixed motorcycle racing with participation in Formula 2 and Formula 3 car races for teams as famous as Matra and Team Lotus, with which he notably managed to beat future champions Jackie Stewart and Jim Clark. However, he missed the motorbike scene and returned to two-wheeled racing eight years later. At the same time, Austrian engineer Harald Bartol, no mean rider in his own right particularly in the 125cc class, would come to gain a legendary reputation as a tuner and engine builder. Described as jocular and modest, but also focussed and determined, Bartol would become the go-to man for up-gunned Yamaha engines in the late 1970s. Over time these modified Yamahas, in the hands mainly of privateers and small teams, were almost unbeatable. For this reason, the marque came to dominate the results table year after year in this decade.

In the early days, reliability had been the chief bugbear of Yamaha privateers. The machines were fast, and in short sprint races were breathtaking. However the more arduous Grand Prix races, over longer distances, presented great problems. A promising young rider at the 1969 TT was Tony Rutter, from Birmingham, who had struggled on the Island in the mid-1960s with Manx Nortons. They had served only to deliver him a string of DNFs. Now, like many others, he had converted to Japanese two-stroke technology. He remembered:

> I had one of the first [Yamaha 350] TRs in 1969 which, like everyone else's would seize up within about seven miles. Still air cooled then with a big front drum brake,

but everyone who wanted to win had bought one – Phil Read had bought one. In the Junior TT it felt like every one but mine had seized up by Ballacraine, but I finished. 14th I think. I thought it was a marvellous bike, another world apart. A 350 or a 500 Manx Norton was just a joke then. Then they were 10 a penny: not now, of course, but they were then; nobody wanted them. Everyone wanted a two-stroke.[1]

His was the third and final Yamaha home in that race. Eight others failed to finish including two entered by the well-known Batley firm of Padgetts, who were Yamaha dealers. Typical of the new breed of privateers was Oxfordshire-born Rod Gould, who built his own machines using Yamaha engines. In 1969 a new race team was formed by the Dutch importers, Yamaha-NV, who signed up the quick and aggressive Gould. He was – typically – a retirement in that year's Lightweight and Junior TT races but things were starting to improve on the reliability front now, and Gould finished second in the scorching hot 1970 Lightweight TT with a modified TD2 production machine, on his way to winning the 250cc World Championship that year. The race was actually won by Australian Kel Carruthers, who was scathing about road surface conditions in the Isle of Man. When he received his prize at the Villa Marina later, he told the audience:

> I am not so concerned about the brick walls and other natural hazards of the TT course. I feel that safety measures could be improved but I consider myself skilled enough not to fall off. My greatest concern is over road conditions which make a mockery of racing. To talk about the Island as a place to develop bikes is merely an excuse … we managed to make the Yamaha behave reasonably well but

... a rider has to exercise more caution than necessary. I found myself more concerned about controlling the bike than going through really fast ... The most enjoyable moment of the 250 race was when I was far enough ahead to slow down. I never stuck my neck out. But I often felt I was going too fast for the road conditions at the places I am worried about. There is no excuse for melting tar. It was warm during TT week but we have roads in Australia unaffected by temperatures in the 80s every day.[2]

Although this was his first and only appearance on the marque at the TT, his was a name that would become synonymous with Yamaha in future years. After the 1970 season he accepted an offer from the firm to race in the United States, where he became tutor to the future world champion Kenny Roberts, and manager of the US Yamaha race team.

Tucked away at the back of the field in the Junior race in 1970 was another face which would become more familiar as the decade progressed. It belonged to a young Yorkshireman with a thick ginger beard. Taking time out from his job as a welder to participate in his first TT, Wakefield's Mick Grant was aboard his sponsor Jim Lee's 350cc TR2, an air-cooled twin-cylinder machine with a wet clutch and a six-speed gearbox. The spine frame was made of 3-inch diameter steel tubing, and although fitted with Seeley forks, the green and orange machine did not handle as well as anticipated, and Grant found that the bike would not fire up first time on starting a race with the plugs hot; the only way to ensure a good start was to replace them on the starting grid with dry plugs. Nevertheless Grant managed to bring home a silver replica for eighteenth place.

Rod Gould had found that with 125cc machines he was less successful, and in the 1971 season his YZ623 was outclassed by Suzuki machinery, but in the 250cc class he was to finish in second place in the World Championship behind Phil Read's privateer Yamaha. Also riding the semi-factory Yamahas at this time was Chas Mortimer, who as an ex-public schoolboy had something of a reputation as a toff, though an extremely popular one all the same. His father had also been a racer in his younger days, and later ran a race school at Brands Hatch. Chas had begun his racing career under the wing of Frank Sheene, with Frank's son Barry as his first mechanic. Mortimer remembered:

> There was a man called Tanaka-san who was Bill [Ivy]'s mechanic ... well Tanaka-san ended up being our liaison with Yamaha motor NV and he approached me at the '71 TT because Rod Gould was concentrating on trying to win the 250 World Championship that year, and he didn't want to ride the 125, the 125 had thrown him down the road at the Austrian Grand Prix when it had broken a conrod and he didn't fancy riding it at the TT. Well I didn't know any of this, because obviously Yamaha used to keep it really quiet, but Tanaka approached me at the TT and he said to me, 'would you be interested in riding our 125 Factory bike' and of course I was obviously wasn't going to say no to that, so we swapped entries and I ended up winning the race for Yamaha, and so they said right we'll concentrate with Rodney on the one on the 250, and you can ride the 125 which is an air-cooled bike and in in all fairness when I got to the Grands Prix it wasn't that competitive, it wasn't that quick and I scored quite a few fourths and fifths with it but never got a Podium on it that first year.[3]

Suzuki-mounted Barry Sheene was also competing in that race, and fell off at Quarter Bridge when he was actually in second place behind Mortimer. Earlier in the week, Sheene had tussled with another Yamaha afficionado, the young, up-and-coming Charlie Williams, already experienced at the Manx Grand Prix and now at his first TT. Williams had grown up close to Oulton Park in Cheshire and from an early age was determined that he wanted to become a professional motorcycle racer, whatever that might take to achieve. It was a determination that would serve him well in his racing career. In the 250cc Production race, Charlie remembered Sheene charging ahead:

> ... unlike me, this was his first time tackling the Mountain Course. [He] made a lightening start to lead the chasing pack down Bray Hill on lap one. I was hard on his heels and although at that stage, I was certainly no expert having only once raced on the course previously in last year's Manx, he seemed to know where he was going, so I followed him until we approached Glen Vine. Now, Glen Vine is a very fast right-hander with a blind approach, the apex can't be seen until you are right on top of it. Never the less, back then 250 Proddy bikes were pretty slow and it wasn't difficult to take it flat in top. For a split second, Barry sat up and shut the throttle, he obviously wasn't too sure where he was. I was very close and had to take quick evasive action and being the first lap, I assumed the riders behind me had to do the same ... I got involved in a bit of a duel with Tommy Robb for second place, but by the end of the first lap I had managed to put some space between us.
>
> I had a trick up my sleeve. We had a large tank fitted to the Yamaha and after practice we calculated that I should be able to do the four laps without a pit stop. Bill [Smith] stopped at the end of lap three but by the time I reached

the end of that lap, he had been and gone. He won the race with me in second place but only ninety seconds behind. Tommy finished third, some two minutes behind me. I was pleased with that result, especially as I got the fastest lap of the race on my final lap.[4]

The 1971 Junior TT was also a dramatic affair. The normally reliable MV Agusta of Giacomo Agostini broke down on the first lap, opening the door to a gaggle of other riders who either broke down themselves or crashed out. Finally, it fell to Seeley-Yamaha mounted Yorkshireman Tony Jefferies to claim the victory. It was the first of Jefferies' three TT wins, though his son David would go on to achieve even greater things two decades later. Mick Grant, riding the Jim Lee-framed Yamaha, finished in seventh place. It was 1971 that also saw the introduction of the 750cc race at the TT, intended to break the domination of the sport by Japanese and Italians, and allow the British factories a way back into the top spot. It was the exclusive preserve at first of BSA and Triumph Triples, and Norton Commandos, but this could not last, and Japanese machines would eventually also come to dominate the Formula 750 TT and its successor, the 1,000cc Open Classic TT, just as they did in the smaller classes.

That year Phil Read was on his own in the World Championships, no longer with the backing of the mighty Yamaha Motor Company behind him. He told those close to him that he had invested all the money he had, some £10,000 (£120,000 in current terms), to buy machines and spares in his bid to secure the championship. This was Read doing what he did best, with his back to the wall and fighting for his very survival in racing, and that year he claimed first place in the Lightweight TT as part of his campaign. Significantly, of the thirty-six riders who completed that race, all but five were Yamaha mounted. Read remembered:

> MZ had recruited Peter Williams to ride the Mountain Circuit, so I knew I'd be in for a tussle. But I also knew there was a question mark over the East German two-stroke's reliability, especially on such a demanding circuit. Obviously the tactic was to try to break the MZ by setting a fast pace from the start in the hope that Peter's bike, when trying to stay with me, would blow up. Off I went at a terrific rate, lapping at more than 100mph from a standing start, and incidentally recording the only ton-topping lap of the race. My tactic worked like a dream. As I pulled in for fuel at the end of the first lap, Peter rolled into view shaking his head disconsolately. When Chas Mortimer's Yamaha went sick too, it looked to be just a matter of finishing to pick up another fifteen points. However, Rod Gould was still out there, climbing through the field, and by the end of the third lap he was up in second place. But a pit stop at the end of the fourth and penultimate lap relegated him to fourth. This lost him vital world championship points, as events would prove.
>
> It was my fifth TT victory, yet strangely enough my first on a 250cc machine. The feeling was still the same, though even if it was my fifth win. No rider can ask for more than to ride to a world championship victory before his home crowd on the tough 37 ¾ mile circuit. The programmes and Union Jacks waved frantically as I went through Governor's Bridge for the last time, weaving round the two slow corners before accelerating down the final straight to the flag. The playing of God Save The

Queen as I stood on the victory podium was fantastic! You can't beat that feeling of achievement.[5]

In the strenuous conditions on the Isle of Man the new extended fairing that he had fitted really proved to be a bonus. The fibreglass now stretched right back to the rear wheel and side panels were placed below the seat. This small touch had the effect of improving aerodynamics; as anything which reduces drag also increases speed. Because Read rightly suspected that the East German machine of Peter Williams would not last the distance, he set off hard. He led from the start and held that position on all four laps. In typical Read style he managed to make his first lap, at over 100mph from a standing start, look both graceful and effortless. Mick Grant was watching the race from the bank at the thirteenth milestone, and remembered that he was always a class act: '… he looked 10mph faster than anyone else yet so smooth and neat … I don't think Read had much by way of technical nous, but on sheer ability he was top drawer, right up there with Hailwood in my book.'[6]

It was Read's first 250cc TT win, but he told reporters afterwards that he had never had it so easy! In reality, the worst problem that he encountered had nothing whatsoever to do with his machine: 'In fact the only unpleasant thing about the race was the smell of onions coming from a hot dog stall at Windy Corner, but I got over that sick-making smell by holding my breath and getting out of range as quickly as possible.'[7]

Read also competed on a 350cc Yamaha that year and for a spell it seemed that he was on course for a double, but he was beset by gremlins, and was forced to retire in the Junior TT when his engine began misfiring due to a possible bearing seizure. His frame was also broken in three places and the chain had jumped the sprocket, a consequence perhaps of not using a stronger Seeley chassis instead of his own, but again reinforcing the point that the TT course with its jumps and bumps was harder on machinery than any other circuit in the world. He was fortunate in securing the services as mechanics that year of Dutchman Ferry Brouwer, and former sidecar world champion and engineer Helmut Fath, from West Germany.

Fath had prepared the engines, and on the 250cc TD2 motor he re-engineered the crank case and changed the balance of the crankshaft. He introduced a dry clutch mechanism which turned out to be invaluable in handling the power of the 350cc engines. The cable operated wet clutch was heavy to use and prone to slip, particularly with the increased power obtained by Brouwer's tuning. After Fath had converted the TR2 to a dry clutch, Phil wanted the 250cc similarly modified. Unfortunately the two engines were completely different, with the 350cc split horizontally and the 250cc vertically. Also the clutches were on opposite sides, so it was not a simple case of repeating the exercise. It was obviously a much more difficult undertaking, and Fath was rather reluctant at first but finally he agreed. Ferry and Helmut spent two evenings discussing how to approach the 250cc, and then undertook the conversion together. To simplify things, an aluminium barrel was built to house the clutch, and keep it separate from the oil in the gearbox; to achieve this, metal had to be machined off some of the gears and shafts to make room for the barrel. Brouwer and Fath added disc brakes to the machines, at that time still a novelty on Grand Prix motorcycles. They also had a six-speed gearbox made by Quaife in Kent to replace the standard five-speed cluster. The 250cc machine was given a Cheney frame (made by Eric Cheney from Reynolds 531 tubing. This new chassis turned out to be 2.25kg lighter than the factory TD2 frame, retaining almost identical geometry to the original item. Only about five or six of these frames were ever built). In addition, a raised visor was placed on top of the windscreen to cope better with the blustery Isle of Man conditions, and electronic ignition added.

Read lifted the 250cc crown, his fifth world title, at Jarama, outside Madrid, at the Spanish Grand Prix. Afterwards he said, 'I have done it all on my own, I gambled every penny I could and it's paid off. I had only myself to look out for and worry about. Everything will be okay from here on in – I'm champion again.'[8]

Before the race, Read had seemed oddly calm. He had so much money at stake that he felt it was his last throw of the dice. Yet these tense circumstances seemed to affect him in exactly the opposite way to what one might expect – just one more puzzle about the man who always seemed to many others to be an enigma. Read remains the only privateer ever to have taken a world title – an astonishing achievement.

Read won the Lightweight TT aboard a 250cc Yamaha again in 1972, it was his sixth Isle of Man victory, and secured more points in the hoped-for defence of his world crown. He described the exciting moment when he caught and passed next-placed man Rod Gould:

> At Quarry Bends I get with them and it is Rodney – leading Derek Chatterton. I make a big effort and get up to Derek's rear wheel on the entry to Sulby Straight. I am obviously hoping for a tow to pull me up to Rod on the works water cooled Yamaha. Slip by, or should I say bounce by, and tuck in behind Rod. But not for long – my God, my bike is faster and I wave goodbye as I take the lead on the road.[9]

He took victory with almost ninety seconds to spare. This was despite the fact that Gould was carrying a specially-made

7-gallon fuel tank which gave him a straight run with no pit stops, whereas Read had pitted for twenty-five seconds at the end of the third lap. The most extraordinary aspect of this race was the help which Read got from other teams. The John Player Norton team had their blue overalled mechanics out around the course in readiness for the afternoon's 750cc race, and they did sterling work in signalling for Read, leaping out at regular intervals to keep him informed. He also received a signal at Ramsey from one of the Yamaha works mechanics – in Japanese!

Chas Mortimer was back at the TT as well, and his earlier success had been noticed by Yamaha; as a result of this, factory parts had started trickling through to him. Often he was among the first to get his hands on something experimental, and this year he was riding the newly introduced water cooled 125cc machine, which proved to be a massive improvement on the 1971 model. Mortimer remembered that was exceptionally good; it was clearly a championship winning bike and under different circumstances that year he should really have won the 125cc world title. In the Ultra-Lightweight TT, however, the prevailing weather was so awful on the day that many argued the race should not even have been run. Mortimer remembered:

> The conditions were as bad as I'd ever known them in the Isle of Man. Very, very poor indeed. Visibility must have been about 20 yards on the Mountain. But I remember believing I was going to win that race right from the start, then I got my first signal and it was minus seven or eight so I thought, 'Well, I'll try a bit harder.' I knew it could only be [Gilberto] Parlotti. By the time he crashed he had pulled out a 30 or 35 second lead and I was trying as hard as I could. I nearly fell off at Sarah's Cottage. I lost the back end big style and really thought I was down. I was

trying so hard and Parlotti was still pulling away – and that was his first TT.[10]

Mortimer finished in first place, but Parlotti was killed in the crash. The incident turned Agostini, and his paymasters at MV Agusta, away from the TT and both vowed never to return to the Isle of Man. Phil Read also declared that he had made his last appearance there, and would no longer risk his life for the sake of 'tradition'. Charlie Williams meanwhile was now beginning to make a name for himself. He now had sponsorship from – among others – Dugdale Motors who were also his employers back home in Cheshire. That year he had six starts at the TT, all on Yamaha machines. He was second behind Mortimer in the 125cc race though he was quite a long way back, as Mortimer's was a factory machine and his was not. In the afternoon he raced in the Senior and finished sixth; it marked the climax of a hectic race week for him, which had included eighteen laps of the Mountain Course in two days.

Another up and coming rider was Tony Rutter, who was celebrating his best result so far at the TT, a second place in the Junior race. Rutter had only turned professional a few months earlier, when he walked away from his job as a tool maker because his employers would not give him time off to go racing. Now he was the proud owner of a *Motor Cycle News* TT100 gold badge, which the newspaper presented at that time to those in the 'ton-up' club. The 30-year-old Rutter told reporters:

> I wanted that ton-up lap badge more than anything. I told Roy, my mechanic, that I'd top 100 mph in Thursday's practice. I know that's unofficial timing but if I'd done it then, I would have been more certain that I could have done it in the race. Unfortunately my gearbox sprung

a leak on the second lap and I stopped on a very oily TD2 Yamaha at the end of a slow lap. After notching a 98.65 mph lap in Wednesday's session, I knew I had the ability to top the ton if conditions were 100 per cent but there were several wet and slippery patches in the race, particularly at Creg-ny-Baa where Charlie Williams fell. I took that one upright on the last lap – my ton up one I thought I'd got round at about 98mph. On the third lap the bike missed three times near Brandywell. After I stopped to refuel, it never missed another beat. I think we might just have been running low on petrol. We'll never know ... When I began to ride Yamahas I thought I'd lap quite easily at over the ton since I'd got round at nearly 98 mph on a Manx Norton. But I was soon down to the 95mph mark – and struggling on the Yam. It took me a long time to learn how to ride the two-stroke. But now, everything seems to have come good.[11]

In 1973 Yamaha introduced a new machine which would have a profound effect on racing worldwide. To the air-cooled TR3 they added plumbing and coolant, and came up with the TZ350. The American magazine *Cycle World* commented:

Unlike most of the world's manufacturers, Yamaha builds genuine roadracing motorcycles in quantity for sale at reasonable prices and this activity has a profound effect on the sport. An entire generation of hot-eyed young riders has learned the roadracer's craft on TD- and TR- series Yamahas. The high knife-edge wail of two stroke engines has become the sound of racing. And our starting fields would be a lot smaller and on average shabbier without the Yamahas ... Yamaha's latest production racer is the TZ

350 and this one should put the RD350 crank and cases to the ultimate test. In most respects the new 350cc racer is just like the '72 TR 350, but the TZ 350 is water cooled. It has a tiny aluminium radiator, a water pump and a one-piece cylinder block with hard-chromed bores. By casting the cylinders together, Yamaha has found room to enlarge the transfer passages and lead them into the cylinders slightly less abruptly, though there has been no change in the port timings. There has been a slight change in expansion chambers but everything else (gear ratios etc) are the same as in the TR 350.[12]

The aluminium radiator was carried in rubber-bushed lugs just below the steering head of the frame, and the water pump was driven by a shaft from the engine. Cylinders for the TZ350 were cast in a block of alloy and contained rather less silicone than the separate hypereutectic cylinders of the TR3. Coolant flowed into the cylinder head through an elbow at the rear and out towards the radiator, past a housing containing a thermostat which held the water temperature at 80°c. There was no red line on the water temperature gauge, but the owner's manual stated somewhat opaquely that 'it is necessary to be careful' above 85°c. It was reported that it was capable of 65mph in first gear, 84mph in second, 113mph in third, 132mph in fourth, 146mph in fifth and 156mph in sixth gear. Around June of 1973 the firm also released the first variant of the TZ250; it too was water cooled, but unlike the TZ350, in this case Yamaha chose to have built-in automatically variable ignition advance in the machine's Hitachi CDI unit. Yamaha also chose to strengthen the main and small-end crank bearings, as well as making a few other minor modifications on the previous TD3.

At the 1973 TT, the absence of the once-dominant Agostini and several other big names opened the door for new faces – and some old ones. Tommy Robb had long since retired from Grand Prix racing, but continued to appear at the TT simply because he loved the Island so much. However, he had always been the bridesmaid, and after fifteen years of competition had never yet stood on the top step of the podium. His chance came out of the blue when Chas Mortimer was injured in the multi-bike pile up at Monza a few days earlier, which had claimed the lives of Renzo Pasolini and Jarno Saarinen. He came to the Island, but was clearly unfit to ride. Mortimer's backer was Danny Keaney, who also happened to sponsor Robb in the Irish races. Before the Ultra-Lightweight race, he contacted Yamaha in Japan and they asked if he could nominate another rider. Thus Robb got the go ahead to ride the 125cc machine. He was relieved that at this stage in his career he was not ranked as one of the top riders, and no one had tipped him to win, which greatly reduced the pressure he was under. He remembered: 'I didn't push the engine for the first six to eight miles because of the new pistons and cylinder. But once I got to Ballacraine the bike felt good and I began to pick up a lot of places.'[13]

Charlie Williams was the hot favourite to win – he set off at number one, whilst Robb was number twelve. He knew that if he could catch Williams on the road, he had a chance, but on the approach to Ramsey the unexpected happened – his main rival came into sight and appeared to be touring. With Charlie now sidelined with mechanical problems, it was Robb's race. He continued:

> I know this seems a startling thing to say, but it's true. Barring an accident or mechanical failure I had the race

won. No one was going to catch me with the machine I had ... I could have lapped at 94mph but it simply wasn't necessary ... However I'll never forget the last lap. When I reached Ramsey I said to myself 'You have got to go over that Mountain.' Then I saw the first programme wavers and was scared to wave back until I reached the Bungalow and realised that spectators would be upset if I didn't acknowledge them. It was a frigid wave which passed from behind my windshield as I headed for home. I was too conscious of all my previous bad luck in the races.[14]

He led from start to finish, and the revitalised Ulsterman finally achieved his dream by taking the win. He even slowed down a little towards the end to give more riders a chance to obtain a replica! One of the first to congratulate him was legendary commentator Peter Kneale of *Manx Radio*, live on air, and at the prize presentation at the Villa Marina *Manx Radio* colleagues carried him on their shoulders to the stage.

The Production 250cc race had seen Maxton-Yamaha rider Williams take his first TT win, with a TD3 machine, and the 1973 Lightweight TT also went to the Cheshire man; he remembered that in the four lap race he set off behind friend and future best man at his wedding, John Williams. It was a humid day with a lot of flies around. Having only one tear-off visor meant that he had to hold on as long as possible before removing it, but when he did it was like someone switching on a light! Charlie had the satisfaction of overhauling his friend on the Mountain and coming home in first place ahead of him. His association with Maxton had come about after some machines which he had been promised by a previous sponsor never materialised:

Just before the start of the season a friend of mine, Ron Williams who was at Maxton – and the name incidentally came from 'Maximum' and 'Ton' as in 100 miles an hour, that's how Maxton was formed – so I got to know Ron through one channel or another, and he'd been an engineer, and he's worked for Chevron Cars, just on the outskirts of Manchester, but he had a big passion for bike racing ... he was a good engineer, he designed and built frames for both the 125 and the 250 Yamahas, so I inherited these bikes. To be honest they weren't very good really, they were worn out by the time I got them, but for the 1973 TT Ron had made a chassis for the TD3 and I raced it and that's what I won on, with the Maxton chassis. When I started winning races, of course other people were saying, 'Well it's got to be these Maxtons' and Ron's order book was full, people like Chas Mortimer, they all wanted Maxtons ... in the early '70s he did have an advantage [over the factory frame]. One of the most important things was I never had anything break on a Maxton chassis, so they were reliable, but the Yamaha ones quite often used to crack around the engine mountings, so you would have to take the engine out, weld them up, reinforce them and so on. Also the wheelbase was slightly longer, and the dimensions a little bit different to the Yamaha, and I think on the road circuits, particularly those such as the Isle of Man, they had a slight advantage there; they did handle very well on circuits like that.[15]

After leader Mick Grant had lost time in the pits fixing just such a broken bracket on his Yamaha, Tony Rutter seized his chance to win the Junior that year, in what was also his first victory. In fact, the race was effectively a Yamaha benefit as besides Rutter the other two steps on the podium were filled by Ken Huggett and John Williams on similar machines. Grant's own 352cc Yamaha had led the 1973 Senior for the first three laps, until he slid off on oil spilled by Rutter in Parliament Square. Before he did so, Grant finally evened the score with outspoken TT commentator Geoff Cannell who was positioned at Ballaugh Bridge. All through practice, Grant had been deliberately landing his TZ front wheel first to spare the chain and transmission from the stress of a rear-wheel landing. To a traditionalist like Cannell this was tantamount to sacrilegious, and he constantly criticised him on air. On the third lap of the Senior, Grant's lead was so great that he was able to take the bridge without the wheels leaving the ground. At the same time he gave a two fingered salute in the direction of the commentary box; Cannell reported that as well as finally getting the bridge right, Grant had even had time to give him a wave!

The TZ350 which Grant rode that year was subjected to close scrutiny in an article in British magazine *Motor Cycle Mechanics*. Calling it a 'Giant Killer', the piece declared:

> There's no doubt about it, to win road races these days you have almost certainly got to ride a Yamaha of one capacity or another … [the TZ350] must be one of the most potent pieces of racing machinery available to the general public … that is if you have greenbacks in your hand to the tune of £1,600 … there's nothing quite like a Yamaha 350 unless it's another Yamaha 350![16]

The track test revealed that with only 2,000 or 3,000 revs on the tachometer, the racing Yamaha 350 reacted like a low powered roadster; but by 5,000rpm, it was obvious that the motor was starting to search for the power band and then at 6,500rpm things really started to happen ... in first, second or third gear the front wheel suddenly went very light, sometimes rising into the air as the machine took off like the proverbial scalded cat. The water cooled engine had a six speed gearbox in comparison with the five speed of the air-cooled model. Consequently, the ratios were closer and rapid shifting in the lower gears was necessary in order to stop the engine over-revving. The power did not start to tail off until the needle reached 11,000rpm, very close to the red line. It could be a difficult machine to handle on a bumpy circuit, tending to take control of a rider until it sorted itself out. Yet in spite of the enormous power output the machine stopped on a sixpence – in the case of Grant's own machine this was in part due to the fact that he had fitted a Ducati hydraulic disc brake, salvaged from a 750cc racer, to the front wheel, the calliper welded directly on to the alloy fork leg. Grant gave his views on the new water cooled model as against the air-cooled version:

> I don't think it's really any faster. And when it comes to reliability, well maybe I've been unlucky and had a bad one ... but the water cooling has caused quite a few problems. In fact 75 percent of my breakdowns this season have been directly connected with the new water cooling system. Perhaps last year's bike was exceptional, but I had far fewer troubles with the early air cooled 350 than I did with this year's job.[17]

Mick also went on to say that in spite of what people might think, the water cooled Yamaha on which he had enjoyed so much success that year was absolutely standard: 'Really it is just a matter of setting them up right. You know, correct jetting, plugs, ignition and gearing ... it can make anything up to 7 to 10 mph difference between two identical bikes!'[18]

Mick remembered that these were the best years of his career; as a privateer with his own two Yamahas in the back of his van, he could make a good living on what he earned travelling from race to race, and without the pressure of a factory team PR machine to please. He recalled that those Yamahas cost very little to maintain and once problems with the water cooling were sorted out they rarely broke down – as he put it, they would go half a season without needing to have a spanner laid on them. Although he didn't finish in the 1973 Senior race, his Yamaha was still subject to a protest that the engine wasn't legal, being under the regulation capacity for that particular class. When it was stripped down the scrutineers decided that it was actually 360cc which was an odd conclusion to come to, but at least on the right side of the fence.

Cylinder capacity was also a consideration in faraway Japan, where Yamaha were beginning work on their first big engine machine. To the outside world, these were the years of high drama on the Grand Prix circuits, dominated by big personalities such as Giacomo Agostini, who would dramatically switch from Italian to Yamaha machinery. Yet behind the scenes, at Yamaha's research department in Japan, these years were no less momentous. They saw the development of the 500 and 750cc machines that were to provide Grand Prix riders with the sheer power they needed in order to trounce their rivals. Just as the 1960s had seen Yamaha gain the advantage in the Lightweight classes, culminating in Phil Read's magnificent double victory with the RA31A 125cc and the RD05A 250cc, so the 1970s were to see them achieve supremacy in the Heavyweight divisions – first with the OW20 YZR500, and then with the 700cc production racer and the 750cc OW31. Coupled with their own engine development, Yamaha bought the revolutionary monocross suspension system that was invented by Belgian Lucien Tilkin. First used on the YZR500 prototype, it was to be installed on all Yamaha's 250, 350, 500 and 750cc machines by 1977.

In mid-October 1973 Yamaha's policy makers met at Hamamatsu to discuss the need for an entry into Formula 750 racing, a class that was growing steadily and which would be afforded the status of a World Championship four years later. It took the board of directors hardly a day to agree unanimously that development of a 750cc machine was essential, and their engineers were given the go ahead to work on a new machine with the necessary engine capacity in order to compete in this class, which was now increasing in popularity in the United States. Not surprisingly for a firm whose reputation was founded on two-stroke technology, it made extensive use of tried and tested components. Its engine used two water-cooled twin-cylinder blocks on common crankcases. The 180° crankshafts were separate, with central gears driving another double-width gear on a countershaft, which connected with the clutch gear on the right. Meanwhile through another pair of gears they rotated the water pump and Hitachi ignition unit on the left side and the clutch gear on the right. Spiral gears from the countershaft drove a gear pump in the sump to force lubrication into the six-speed gearbox. A user-friendly touch was that the gear-change shaft projected out of each side of the cases, so that linkages were unnecessary to switch sides.

With their reputation as successful two-stroke manufacturers to maintain, Yamaha now wanted a big capacity machine to acts as a flagship for their otherwise successful squadron. At a time when big, beefy motorcycles were hitting peaks of demand, world-wide publicity in this field was vital. Developed by Naito and the team responsible for the 500, the 700cc racer was breathtaking. Catalogued the TZ750, it was closely allied to the

YZR500, modified only to increase the piston displacement. The four-cylinder engine with seven ports and a suction system with a piston reed valve, consisted of two-cylinder blocks. The TZ750 was the first Yamaha road-racing motorcycle to feature reed valve induction, a measure considered necessary to broaden what would otherwise have been an unacceptably peaky power delivery. The bore and stroke were 64 x 54mm, similar to that of the TZ350. The engine was equivalent to that of the TZ350 doubled up, in fact its engine looked like two TZ350 twins on a common crankcase, although in actuality few components were shared. The crankshaft, piston and other parts were all similar to those of the TZ350, although these parts were also not interchangeable. With the same 64 x 54mm internal dimensions as the 350cc twins, the capacity actually came out at only 694cc and the factory designation of this early prototype was in fact TZ700A. When the machine was revealed at the 1973 Tokyo motorcycle show, the racing world was stunned.

Because the transmission system was similar to that of the YZR500, it used a gear in the middle of the crankshaft. Power went through a dry sump to the six-stage transmission through the driveshaft and the multi-plate clutch. The engine rotated anti-clockwise for forward direction, because power was transmitted through the idler shaft. The magneto, water pump and oil pump for the transmission – situated on the left side of the bike – were all driven through the idler shaft. These components went into an entirely new, twin-shock frame that looked reminiscent of the Rob North-designed chassis used by the racing BSA-Triumph 750 Triples. At 10,000rpm the bike was said by technicians at the time to be giving better than 90bhp and a speed in excess of 175mph. In fact, it was capable of returning 130bhp, but the tyres and chains could not stand the excessive strain that this put on them, and so

Yamaha were forced to detune it. In October 1974 Yamaha produced an improved version of the TZ750. This was a full-size 748cc model, with a top speed in excess of 175mph, and was designated TZ750B. The works model, code named YZR750, weighed only 160kg, 10kg less than the production machine. The 66.4 x 54 mm cylinders delivered a maximum of 110hp in the works machine and 100hp in the production bike, achieved at around 10,000rpm. The main area of improvement, other than in capacity, was in handling: the works machines were fitted with the new monocross suspension at the rear end, though the production TZ750s retained the standard suspension.

Although Formula 750 had been intended as a class for modified production road bikes, Yamaha managed to get its purpose-built TZ750 racer homologated provided that at least 200 were built. Like the smaller TZ twins, the TZ750 was an enormous success, providing privateers the world over with the means to compete against the factory teams in Formula 750. Packed grids of near-identical bikes made for close racing, and no-one who witnessed these demanding machines being wrestled around UK short circuits, the Isle of Man TT course, or Daytona's bumpy banking would ever forget the sight. Because Yamaha only ever made slightly fewer than 800 of these spectacular motorcycles, today they are highly sought after by collectors and classic racers alike. Conceived at a time when rising power outputs were often more than factory frames and suspension could cope with, the TZ750 inevitably attracted the attentions of the aftermarket frame-makers, the foremost in the field certainly being Cheshire-based Maxton Engineering. Started in 1971 by Ron Williams, a legend in the world of chassis and suspension design, Maxton frames and (later) suspension units were, and still are, regarded as among the best there is.

In 1976 Yamaha would introduce the OW31, which was the ultimate four-cylinder 750. This was the final factory version of the TZ750, ridden by the likes of Steve Baker and Kenny Roberts at World Championship level. Motor-wise the bike had six transfer ports per cylinder, unlike the stock TZ750 model. Other improvements over the customer 750's were copious amounts of titanium and magnesium, in order to save 18kg in weight, and a mono-shock frame. It got better season by season and continued to evolve until 750cc racing ceased in 1979. It came to be the yardstick by which other 750cc machines were measured.

The 1977 TZ750D was marketed by Yamaha as a 'works' OW31 replica, and as a result a high percentage of those who now own one like to claim their machines are OW31's, when in fact they are little more than a mono-shock TZ750C with mufflers – an incredibly powerful machine none the less. None of the exotic metals or components from the OW31 were used on the over-the-counter TZ750D, for the obvious reason of keeping costs down. The only changes to the motor were alterations to the pistons, exhaust ports, jetting, crankshafts and ignition wiring. Other components to receive an upgrade were the exhausts, which now had the left hand outer pipe twisting around behind the carbs to allow the chambers underneath the motor to be the correct round section. The exhausts were also now fitted with silencers, and the frame bracing was increased. Only about twenty or so *genuine* OW31's were produced that year, and just ten more TZ750Ds making a total of thirty. The D model sold for £7,000 (about £39,000 today) including a spares kit.

Opinion differs on what the TZ750 was like to ride competitively. Some claim that it was vicious and unpredictable. On a TZ350 the sudden and intoxicating rush of power could at least be kept under control simply because it was much lighter, but the big four was in another league, with corners rushing up – and looking increasingly narrow – at frightening speeds. The engine's smoothness cloaked its evil intentions too, beguiling the rider into the feeling that it could be tamed. Others by contrast thought that it was akin to riding a diesel motorcycle – strong but sedate. It was the most powerful production motorcycle that had ever been offered for sale up to that point, and one of the first riders in the UK to get his hands on one was Chas Mortimer. It was imported into the UK by his sponsor Danfay's Danny Keaney. For Mortimer, that TZ750 proved to be a money spinner, even though the Formula 750 class had yet to be officially ratified by the FIM for another year. For about £4,000 he had a race ready machine with spares to last most of a season including two spare cylinder blocks, two crankshafts, six pistons, clutch plates, carb spares, sprockets and even a modest tool kit. He remembered: 'That bike made me a lot of money, it was ideal for the European circuits because it was so easy to ride. Others thought it difficult, but I was lucky with the handling.'[19]

Yet the machine seems to have been little used on the Isle of Man. Perhaps the Island's twisting Mountain Circuit was not well suited for its characteristics and – with a few notable exceptions – most Yamaha riders preferred to use the ubiquitous TZ350 for Manx racing instead, and this model would go on to dominate the smaller classes on the Island for the remainder of the 1970s.

Chapter Four

1974–1981
THE TZ YEARS

By the mid-1970s the Isle of Man TT had seen a new wave of riders come to the fore. With the departure of heavyweights such as Phil Read and Giacomo Agostini, younger riders such as Mick Grant, Charlie Williams, Chas Mortimer and Tony Rutter had been given the chance to shine and show the racing public exactly what they were capable of. Almost invariably these riders were equipped with Yamaha machines and one model in particular – the TZ350 – would come to dominate the starting grid at the TT for the remainder of the 1970s. The Yamaha marque would also be the preferred choice for an old hand returning to the TT for the first time in over a decade – and for a newcomer who would go on to become the most successful racer in TT history.

For many riders, it was the sheer versatility and ease of maintenance of the TZs that made them attractive. It was a Dugdale Maxton Yamaha TZ385 (an over stroked 350cc machine) that would take Charlie Williams to a pair of second places in two Isle of Man TT races just five days apart: the Formula 750, and the Senior TT, as well as tenth place in the 1974 500cc World Championship on the back of that, and his fifth place finish in the Dutch TT at Assen three weeks later. Williams had been turned down by the organisers when he applied for a ride at the Dutch TT the previous year, so this was evidence of his growing experience and reputation as a racer. The machine was something of a 'bitser' that Dugdale had put together, based on an engine built by Dutch engineer Cees van Dongen. It used some components from a Yamaha road bike, such as RD400 conrods, as well as a TR2 crank which had a longer stroke, so for the same bore they could take the cylinder capacity up to 385cc. Charlie remembered:

> Those TZs, the 250 and the 350 engines, particularly the 350, they were incredible engines ... and they still are, they're still out there, doing their thing. Yamaha were the only ones who really made a production racer that you could buy, they were relatively cheap ... and spares were relatively cheap, and everyone used them. They powered everything. It was a pity really because that immediately almost sounded the death knell for the Manx Nortons and G50s and such, because we could get eccentric crank pins turned up [for the Yamaha] ... to make them eligible for the 500 class, [for which] they needed to be 351 plus. So you put some eccentric crank pins in, and another base gasket under the cylinder and you've got yourself a 351 which is eligible.[1]

His 700cc Yamaha however had fallen foul of the Manx scrutineers during practice week, when they objected to an aerofoil fitted to the fairing above the front wheel, intended to help keep it on the ground. They pointed to a regulation banning such additions, but entrant Alan Dugdale argued that in the interests of safety, some sort of fin or wing like this would certainly become necessary in the future because of the sheer power output of these big machines. Charlie however was rather wary of the bigger-engined Yamahas, having been thrown off one at Oulton Park earlier in the month, and for the Isle of Man at least he confined himself to smaller capacity machines.

The 1974 Junior TT was again Tony Rutter's, as he won the event for the second year running on a Bob Priest Yamaha, the Stourbridge businessman having been a loyal backer for Rutter since 1969. Yet it was a lonely race as he told reporters afterwards:

> I simply hated the idea of being first away. If there is one thing I have been dreading all week it is putting that number one on my machine. It gets so lonely out there in the front. I like to be with a good bloke so that it is possible to have a good race. It is far easier to pace yourself in conditions like that. I did not realise what was going on during the race as far as the others were concerned. I know now of course and it feels marvellous to have won again. I could not have asked for any more luck. I did not realise that Charlie Williams was leading the race until I came in for my pit stop at the end of the third lap. It was then that my mechanics told me of the situation. It was the same thing about Charlie Mortimer. I did not know he was so close until he pulled in for fuel at the same time as me. Then as I went into Crosby someone held out a board that simply read 'number one.' From this I gathered that something had gone wrong for Chas and this was confirmed when I got a signal up on the mountain. All I knew was that I was in with a chance if I kept going.
>
> There was not much to report about the race. The machine went well and the only problem was the front brake which gave trouble from the first lap. I had to pump it to make it operate properly. I did have a fuel reserve in the tail of the seat with a tap just below the seat on the

right hand side. I tried to switch it on during the third lap but was not able to do so. Once I did get the message that I was in the lead I got that dreaded feeling on the last lap that something might go wrong. It really is a terrible feeling especially when you are comfortably ahead. Even though I won last year there is always the feeling that you will never be lucky enough to be on the winner's rostrum two years running. It's marvellous.[2]

In 1974 Mick Grant picked up two Yamaha rides at the TT when a fellow rider was injured. He remembered that with his own right wrist in plaster from an injury at Brands Hatch he had to roll the throttle on and off as if rolling pastry – event organisers today would never allow one rider out onto the race track with such a disability, never mind two, but Charlie Williams was also sporting a similar injury from his 750cc get-off whilst battling with Barry Sheene at Oulton Park a week earlier. Mick remembered:

> The broken wrist still wasn't 100 per cent, but on the smaller bikes not too big a handicap, and I was well pleased with second place in the Junior albeit miles behind Tony Rutter who lapped at a brilliant 106mph. Wednesday's 250cc TT was an utter shambles which brought a similar result on the Fowler Yamaha. Rain and bad visibility caused the start to be delayed by hours, when we finally did get away, Charlie Williams disappeared into a lead he never lost. Mind you he had an edge – only his left wrist was in plaster. This left me to dice for second place with Chas Mortimer.
>
> This was all going to plan when I went into the Creg a bit too hot with the back wheel hopping and skittering

and buried the front end in the bales. As I landed I turned round to see Chas riding past with a big grin on his face. Chas was a lovely bloke but a bit of a toff and a bounder who always reminded me of Terry Thomas. I cursed a bit, dragged the TZ from under the bales and set off again. On the drop down to Brandish I could smell burning rubber, so something was obviously bent but by the time I got to Hillberry it seemed to have gone, so I just thought 'bugger it' and carried on.

After a once-over at the pits I got my head down, and found myself promoted to third place ... I was pushing hard – my last lap was the fastest of the race – but had more or less settled for third when who should I see pushing out of Governor's Dip but dear old Chas. Apparently his filler cap was leaking and he'd run out of fuel. 'Take that you bounder,' I thought. 'Now it's my turn to grin.'[3]

In those days however, having a broken wrist whilst riding was not such a handicap as one might think. In the early 1970s it was not common for riders to hang off the bike with a knee down for corners, in the style which Barry Sheene had made fashionable by the end of the decade. Certainly photographs of Williams from this era illustrate his economical riding style, which involved staying seated on the bike with knees tucked in. In this position, he would not have had to put extra weight on his damaged wrist in order to lever himself from side to side on the bike when cornering. However, the disadvantage of staying seated on the bike when going into turns is that it is necessary to get more lean angle, in order to carry the speed through the corner. For this reason, the Maxton frame incorporated footrests which perhaps seem high by later standards.

Williams considered himself something of a wet roads specialist, so that gave him a certain advantage in the 250cc race, but he also thought himself fortunate in that the favourite for this class, his pal John Williams had been sidelined following a spill in practice week. The race brought him his third TT win, but it was not without drama as Charlie recounts:

> There was something quite new to me for the '74 TT. I had started wearing glasses whilst racing. Having won the 250 race the previous year, I was allocated start number one and as John [Williams] had been due to start alongside me, I sat on the start line alone. It was raining quite heavily, so much so that, unusually for me, I opted to wear a waterproof oversuit. As the starter was about to climb on his platform, I pulled down my visor. Shock horror! I could hardly see a thing. As usual, I had spent time applying anti-mist (Fairy Liquid) to the visor but I forgot about the glasses! My mechanic, Eddy, was just leaving the start line. I shouted to him and he turned around. I beckoned him to come back. He looked confused. I had already snatched the glasses from my face and handed them to Eddy. He looked shocked but there was no time for discussion as within seconds the flag had dropped, and I was away. The conditions suited me, and with an opening lap some 32 seconds faster than Mick [Grant] and Chas Mortimer, I went on to win comfortably.[4]

History was made in the Thursday of race week that year, when Phil Carpenter won Yamaha's first ever Senior TT. Having started in fair conditions, the weather during the race rapidly deteriorated. Up on the Mountain things were wet and windy that day, meaning that the duration of the race was shortened.

Carpenter, a 26-year-old fork lift truck driver from Rixton near Warrington was never out of the first two placings. Racing in only his second TT, he secured his place in the history books by bringing his 351cc twin home in first place. For the first two laps it was Charlie Williams who dominated, but worsening conditions and reduced visibility put paid to his chances – his visor had begun to mist up and there was little that he could do about it. Williams admitted that even though he considered himself to be a wet weather specialist, Carpenter was having the ride of his life that day. Another potential challenger, Mick Grant, retired at Ballacraine when his 351cc Yamaha encountered gearbox trouble early on, and the machine kept jumping out of gear. Chas Mortimer also looked promising with a quick early fuel stop, but at Ballaugh on lap two his Yamaha seized. At the end of the race, Carpenter confessed to reporters that he had not initially believed that he had much of a chance, but things just fell right for him. As both Williams and Carpenter were part of the Dugdale team, the Cheshire outfit also carried off the manufacturer's award for this race. Although he competed for a further three years, this was the high point of Carpenter's career and he did not win another TT. All agreed that the conditions that day were among the worst ever experienced.

Mortimer had better luck on the Friday when he won the Formula 750 event. However he almost didn't start the race after a coil burned out on his 350cc Danfay Yamaha – the same machine that was ridden by Grant in the Junior TT – as the machines were brought to the start line. Mechanics managed to change it with seconds to spare, and he got away. The weather was changeable – in parts of the course it was raining, and in others dry, but the track was damp. The wind was also strong and variable. It was a day for privateers, as the conditions did

Right: Taneharu Noguchi in action in the 1961 Lightweight TT. (Courtesy of Manx National Heritage PG/12100/40)

Below left: Tony Godfrey at the 1963 Lightweight TT. Shortly after this photo was taken he came off, and was seriously injured. He was the first rider at the TT to be helicoptered to hospital. (Fottofinders)

Below right: Phil Read, who joined the Yamaha team in 1963. (Author's Collection)

Above: The 1965 Lightweight TT podium: Redman (Honda), Duff (Yamaha), and Perris (Suzuki). (Fottofinders)

Left: Bill Ivy, Read's team mate at Yamaha. A bitter rivalry soon developed between the two. (Author's Collection)

Above: Phil Read at the start of the 1968 Lightweight TT. (Author's Collection)

Right: Australian Kel Caruthers, winner of the 1970 Lightweight TT. (Author's Collection)

Rodney Gould, who rode for Yamaha-NV, the Dutch importer's team. (Courtesy of Ken Sprayson)

Rod Gould's 1971 250cc Lightweight TT machine, in the colours of Yamaha-NV, being pushed through the warm up area by mechanic Nobby Clarke. (Author's Collection)

Phil Read (no 6) pushes his privately entered Yamaha away from the line in the 1971 Lightweight TT, on his way to winning the 250cc World Championship. (Fottofinders)

Charlie Williams in the 1972 Production TT. He finished second behind John Williams. (Author's Collection)

The 1973 Ultra-Lightweight podium. Winner Tommy Robb at the centre. (Fottofinders)

John Williams in the 1973 250cc Lightweight TT. In this race Williams finished second behind fellow Cheshire rider Charlie Williams. (Author's Collection)

Tony Rutter (no 10) versus John Williams in the 1973 Junior TT. Rutter won, with Williams in third. The top twenty-one places in this race were filled by Yamaha machinery. (Author's Collection)

Above: Mick Grant pushes his Yamaha off the line in the 1973 Junior TT. (Author's Collection)

Left: Bob Heath aboard a 250cc Yamaha in 1974. He finished in twenty-fifth place in the Lightweight TT. (Courtesy of Ken Sprayson)

Chas Mortimer, Danfay Yamaha, warming up for the 1974 Ultra-Lightweight TT. Chas retired in the race. (Courtesy of Ken Sprayson)

Barry Randle, from Stourbridge, awaiting the start of the 1974 Junior TT. His Padgetts Yamaha was a retirement in this race. (Courtesy of Ken Sprayson)

Dick Greasley and Cliff Holland, Chell Yamaha, in action in the 1975 1000cc Sidecar TT. (Courtesy of Ken Sprayson)

Percy Tait, who was briefly a Yamaha development rider and who took a 750cc machine to second place in the 1975 Classic TT. (Courtesy of Ken Sprayson)

George O'Dell, in pensive mood at the 1977 TT. (Courtesy of Ken Sprayson)

Joey Dunlop's first TT victory; the 1977 Jubilee event. Little-known at that time, Dunlop (Rea Racing) shook the TT regulars by taking victory in this one-off race on his home-built Seeley-framed Yamaha. (Fottofinders)

The 1978 TT Martini Yamaha line-up. Ted Macauley stands second left, whilst mechanic Nobby Clarke stands third right. Mike Hailwood at the centre. (Courtesy of Ted Macauley)

George Fogarty on the Sports Motorcycles Yamaha lines up alongside Mike Hailwood, at the start of the 1978 Classic TT. (Courtesy of Ken Sprayson)

Start of the 1978 Classic TT – number 5 is Maxton Yamaha mounted Bill Smith. (Courtesy of Ken Sprayson)

Charlie Williams, Maxton Yamaha, before the 1979 Senior TT. (Courtesy of Ken Sprayson)

Ron Haslam would be a big name with Honda in the 1980s, but began his career with Maxton framed Pharaoh Yamahas. He is seen here in preparation for the 1979 Junior TT. (Courtesy of Ken Sprayson)

Jock Taylor and Benga Johanssen, in action in the 1981 Sidecar B TT. (Courtesy of Ken Sprayson)

Taylor and Johanssen celebrate after victory in the 1981 Sidecar B race. (Courtesy of Ken Sprayson)

not suit the generally bigger engined works machines. It was a Battle Royale between Mortimer and Charlie Williams, who set the fastest lap of the race (and also fastest lap of the week). By the end, Mortimer had an oil leak and Tony Rutter on the Junior TT-winning 350 Yamaha was gaining on him, but Mortimer came in with eight seconds to spare ahead of Williams. He added after the win:

> Plans do work! My sponsor Danny Keaney, and I worked out a simple plan for the 750cc TT – it was just Plan F – for finish. Finish we did and it was marvellous to win. Paul Smart passed me shortly after Bray Hill on the opening lap. I tried to hang on but I couldn't see him by Crosby village. It wasn't the type of conditions to take chances. My safety margins were wide. My only worry was soon before the off when a coil went duff. But the lads sorted things out OK.[5]

Keaney's Dublin-based company Danfay had held a franchise for Yamaha distribution since 1965, although it was not just motorcycles that they dealt with. They also handled musical instruments, speedboats, and anything else that the Yamaha Corporation produced. Although the Yamaha factory no longer raced directly on the Isle of Man, they could not resist putting out a cheeky press release drawing attention to the success of their machines, in the wake of Rutter's win in the Junior; they must have been absolutely delighted by the end of the 1974 TT, when Mortimer's victory gave the firm a tally of five outright solo wins plus the 250 section of the Production event.

On the Tuesday of race week in 1975 came the rain-delayed Senior TT. It proved to be an epic battle between Kawasaki-mounted Mick Grant and the Yamaha of John Williams. As the race unfolded the lead swapped between them, but in the end it was Grant's Kawasaki which proved superior. Chas Mortimer finished third, whilst Charlie Williams was seventh. In 1975 Manchester-based frame wizard Ron Williams had brought five cantilever versions of his Maxton chassis to the TT – two each to be ridden in the Junior and Senior by Eddie Roberts and Charlie Williams, and the other, in a distinctive red colour by Chas Mortimer. The frames weighed the same as standard Maxtons and used Armstrong racing car suspension units, internally modified by Williams. It was the single suspension unit, rather than the cantilever frame, which was chiefly responsible for their improved handling and roadholding. There was no difficulty with balancing the units, since each frame had only one, and each unit could be modified to give the ideal desired characteristics. Rear wheel movement was improved from 3 to 5 inches, and as a result the wheel followed the contour of the road much better. The new frames had been tested at Oulton Park prior to the TT, with very promising results. Ron Williams told reporters:

> The bike rides the bumps much better, is more stable and the tyres stick to the road better. One of the first things we noticed was the way the exhaust note stayed constant over the bumpy bits instead of the revs soaring like the standard bike. This is because the back wheel is staying in contact with the road and not allowing the revs to rise. I think the cantilever frame will be a big advantage in the Isle of Man because it will reduce rider fatigue. The testers have said they just cannot feel the bumps.[6]

In the event, that first monoshock frame which Ron produced worked so brilliantly straight out of the box, that Charlie Williams won the 1975 Junior TT on it. Conditions were excellent for the race and as he pushed away from the line alongside

Tony Rutter all eyes were on the duo, expecting a fierce battle to unfold. Tom Herron led on the road but behind him Alex George and Chas Mortimer were jostling for position. By the Bungalow however, Williams was in the lead. By the end of lap two, in almost unprecedented situation it was a dead heat between Williams and George, both on identical times. By the following lap Williams had edged very slightly ahead, but by the time George pulled into the pits unofficial timing had him one second in the lead. On the fourth lap at Ballaugh Bridge it had changed again, with commentator Geoff Cannell reporting that Williams now had a four second advantage over George. At the Bungalow Charlie was using all of the road in a bid to stay ahead, his knee down as he took the swooping series of bends on the approach to the tram lines. In the last lap, Tommy Robb in the commentary box at Ballacraine reported that Williams was pulling away from George in what was turning out to be one of the most dramatic races in TT history. On the last lap, with some ten seconds in hand Williams acknowledged the applause of the crowd with a wave. So hard was Alex George riding that he slid off on the final run down the Mountain, though he was not seriously injured. Charlie remembered:

> Alex George and I had a tremendous Junior race ... [we] slugged it out with only seconds between us. He set the fastest lap of the race at 106.29 on his second lap and when we came in to refuel at the end of the lap we had both averaged 104.91 mph for those two laps. I had managed to pull out a six second advantage by the start of the fifth and final lap, but poor Alex hit problems on that lap and eventually crashed at the 33rd milestone. For the record, Chas Mortimer finished second with Tom Herron in third place.[7]

It was yet another all-Yamaha podium, and chatting with Peter Kneale in the winner's enclosure afterwards Charlie agreed that conditions had been pretty much ideal, his only concern was that at Quarter Bridge and Parliament Square the sidecar drivers had left quantities of oil on the road! Although the marshals had put copious amounts of cement dust down, it was still very dangerous. He had none the less been confident of going fast, because he knew from the previous year's performance just what the Yamaha was capable of. To underline the camaraderie which existed between riders, he revealed that one of his signalling stations was actually being operated by the wife of third placed man Tom Herron.

The six-lap 1975 1,000cc Classic TT took place on the Friday of race week. By now it had usurped the Senior as the big-bike, big money finale to the TT fortnight, with a £1,500 first prize (nearly £15,000 today) and it was won in fine style this year by John Williams on Gerald Brown's 350cc Yamaha. Although he had scored podiums previously on Yamaha machinery, this was the first time one of their motorbikes had taken him to the top spot. Brown meanwhile was one of the biggest sponsors in British motorcycle racing in the mid-1970s. A second hand car dealer from Rugely in the West Midlands, he was also chairman of the Sponsors' Association, and at various times had also given financial backing to Barry Sheene and Charlie Williams. He was quick to point out that for many sponsors like himself, their business did not directly benefit from motorcycle racing, and their investment in the sport was really just a hobby, albeit an expensive one! He told reporters:

> I feel that 250cc and 350cc racing is more exciting than any other kind. The machines are relatively cheap to maintain and they provide an excellent spectacle ... I sponsor

these types of machines and I'm sure they are the racing machines of the future.[8]

Charlie Williams had confirmed before the race that he would be riding the same 350cc Yamaha that had taken him to victory in the Junior outing earlier in the week, albeit with a different crankshaft and some other modifications. Hot favourite for the race beforehand was Mick Grant, whose Kawasaki machinery was sweeping all before it this year; John Williams for his part was unfancied because of a partly healed broken collar bone, the result of a multi-bike pile-up at the Austrian Grand Prix a few weeks earlier, and it left him in pain throughout the race. The event was run in glorious weather – always beneficial to lap times. From the start Grant was on a record-breaking schedule, but shared the early lead with the equally fast 'works' 750cc Yamaha four of Percy Tait, which had previously seen action in the 750cc World Championship series in the hands of Finnish rider Tepi Länsivuori. Grant soon opened a gap between himself and Tait, and in the process shattered Mike Hailwood's outright lap record set eight years earlier, but the Kawasaki could not withstand the pace, and Grant retired later in the race. Tony Rutter, on Rob Priest's Offenstadt framed 350cc Yamaha, was not among the early challengers but soon pulled up to third place after a quicker pit stop than John Williams.

With Grant out the two 350cc Yamahas now battled for the lead. Rutter too went out after his chain broke at Ballaugh Bridge, leaving Williams way out in front, several minutes ahead of Tait. In the end however he had to coast home, having run out of fuel 250 yards from the finish line. He told reporters afterwards: 'I took a look into the tank near the Bungalow on the last lap. The tank looked dry but there was enough still in the well to be ok, I took it steady from then and made certain.'[9]

Veteran Percy Tait admitted that his big TZ750 machine, which he nicknamed 'Leaping Lena' was a handful. The steering damper had broken in the warming up area, and this had by no means improved its handling. Tait was at this time employed by Yamaha as a test and development rider, trying to resolve some of the problems inherent in the 750, and was travelling between Amsterdam and Japan to offer his advice. He remembered: 'We'd got it sorted out by October and the revised model was in the shops by April. They were super people to work with, so efficient at getting things done.'[10]

Other exotic machinery in this race included the TZ750A ridden by Chester motor trader Bill Smith. This machine had previously been ridden to victory by Gene Romero at Daytona, his only success at that iconic race, in March of 1975. Shortly after its Daytona victory the bike was purchased by Bill Smith, together with a number of other competition machines, from Yamaha US race team boss Kel Carruthers in April 1975. Actually displacing just 694cc, its water-cooled two-stroke four-cylinder engine produced 90bhp at 10,500rpm. Equipped with twin rear shock absorbers, its swing-arm frame also housed a six-speed gearbox. Weighing just 157kg, it proved to phenomenally quick but this version was already on the way to being obsolete when it raced on the Isle of Man, due to the introduction the following year of the even faster 'B' variant.

It was before the next year's TT, in 1976, had even started however that a potential problem with the newly introduced Yamaha TZ-C monoshock frames came to the fore. This model, which was only just becoming widely available, was a radical departure in terms of chassis and running gear from the earlier TZ models. Adjustable 'mono-shock' (spring preload and rebound damping only) rear suspension, combined with twin piston front and rear disk brakes made this machine a must-have, with the new bikes selling like hot-cakes from Yamaha dealers worldwide. The retail price of around £1,550 including a comprehensive spares kit, was highly affordable and boosted sales. The clutch basket 'boss' was improved by changing the method of attachment to a male/female spline system, compared with the 'dog' type on the previous model. The exhaust header picked up an additional O-ring and a new mounting system. Power had jumped up slightly to 62bhp at 10,000rpm.

Glasgow-born roads specialist Alex George arrived on the Island to inform scrutineers that in his experience, and that of several other riders, the new TZ350 frames had a tendency to develop a crack which started on the support stays for the swing arm pivot. The fixing would then work loose and crack the arm itself, which could then break up entirely. George also had a warning about brake pads in the same type of machine, which when worn down had a tendency to shoot out of the calliper.

No such problems presented themselves in the first race of the week however, the 1976 Production TT, run on Saturday, 5 June. This was mainly because most of the field were basically modified road bikes. Danfay Distributors, who were the Yamaha importers for the Republic of Ireland, had entered Chas Mortimer and Billy Guthrie on an RD400 in the 500cc class. At short notice Chas Mortimer changed to ride (and win) the ten lap race on an RD250 with Bill Simpson, father of Ian. In a curious twist of fate (beloved by TT trivia fans everywhere) an as yet unknown Joey Dunlop from Ballymoney took over the berth vacated by Mortimer. In the event, Guthrie retired on only the first lap, which is how Joey also came to be listed as a retirement in his first TT, without ever even getting aboard the motorcycle!

Dunlop however had been gaining skill and confidence over the previous two years in Irish racing, with a succession of Yamahas. By now he had come to the attention of John Rea of Rea Transport, one of the biggest sponsors in Northern Ireland. The relationship would grow into one of mutual respect and affection, and John Rea would come to be like a second father to Joey right up to the time that he eventually went to ride for Honda. In those early days, Rea decided that Joey needed a better bike, and bought a new TZ350 and Seeley frame, the better to cope with the bumpy conditions on Irish circuits. Eventually Joey would end up with three bikes – 250, 350 and a 351cc '500' – all with Seeley frames. In the early days at the TT, Joey and his crew (the infamous Armoy Armada) would stay at former Irish racer Norman Dune's guesthouse, the Walpole, at 1 Hutchinson Square, Douglas. It was known to all as the Irish Embassy, and was famous for the sheer quantity of booze which went in the front door.

Two days after the Production event came Chas Mortimer's most satisfying victory, in the 1976 Junior TT when he lapped at over 108mph, and was in command of the race virtually from start to finish, without really being pushed. With his Danfay Team Sarome Yamaha he smashed lap and race records on the way, and remembered: 'It was one of those days when everything went right. I knew when I got to the morning that no-one but me was going to win that 350cc TT. Silly really because Tony Rutter was riding very well.'[11]

It was his seventh TT victory and he built up such a commanding lead in the opening stages that he was easily able to fend off a late challenge from Tony Rutter. Rutter for his part had experienced problems in the first lap from a leaking filler cap on his Yamaha, but had a better run on the second circuit when he set his own lap record of 108.69mph. Mortimer told reporters afterwards:

I didn't seem to be travelling at record breaking speeds. I'm not saying it was an easy race, but it certainly was not a hard one for me. The Yamaha was going well and I must admit I did feel rather confident of success. I set off at what I thought was the sort of pace that would be required with people like Tom Herron, Alex George and Tony Rutter about, and of course I did not know that Tony was having problems with petrol getting on to his leathers. Conditions were ideal and the records just had to go but it certainly did not feel as though I was going round so quickly.

I took a long time over the pit stop because I always like to be certain that I have got plenty of fuel. I don't like to chance on that score. I always insist on having more fuel than is necessary, much to the annoyance and alarm of my mechanic.[12]

Once he began the final lap he was confident he would win if the machine kept going. The only minor mechanical problem that he did encounter was that the clutch adjustment started to go, no doubt because a new one was fitted, and two cracks in the Maxton frame, in the front down tube near the engine mounting (which had been brazed up the night before the race) had reappeared.

Fellow competitor Charlie Williams almost missed the start – he had flown to Italy at the end of practice week to take part in an endurance race. His plane for the return trip suffered mechanical problems and was delayed as a result. Racer John Williams picked him up at Ronaldsway and he got into his leathers in the car on the way to the Grandstand. To his dismay as he approached the start line he could hear the roar of machines starting off. Charlie had been due to lead the riders away, but race officials hearing what had happed allowed him to start at the back of the field. Amazingly he fought his way up through the pack to second place, and Mick Grant, who was without a ride in the Junior, was watching from the top of Barregarrow. He recounts how the rest of the field rolled back the throttle or changed gear for this bend, but not Charlie! He came through in top gear, absolutely flat out with his chin on the tank; but it was all to no avail, as his race was ended by a water leak.

Chas Mortimer, who earlier in the week had been quite confident of his chances in the Senior, became less so as it approached. Following his success in the Junior, he felt that the 354cc Yamaha that he was due to ride was not going to be quick enough to outpace the opposition, and so it was to prove. The 1976 Senior TT was held on the Wednesday of race week, and was won by Tom Herron aboard a Yamaha TZ-C with a 354cc engine, as was the Lightweight TT with a similar TZ250C. Like its bigger brother, the new model featured a monoshock chassis, with the rear shock featuring adjustable pre-load and rebound damping, as well as disc brakes front and rear. In terms of the motor, the factory had chosen to pursue ease of riding, rather than outright horsepower. Revised porting comprising wider intake and transfer ports with altered angles of entry, raised compression and a new exhaust achieved this for them to a certain degree. The exhaust was mounted on newly designed brackets, and the clutch basket 'boss' to primary driven gear attachment was improved by changing from previous model's 'dog' teeth to a female spline, this of course required the primary driven gear to be altered to utilise a male spline.

Run in perfect conditions for racing, the Senior turned out to be a repeat of that the previous year – hot favourite John Williams had led from start almost to finish, but ran out of petrol on the final lap as had to coast in. He resorted to pushing the machine 1 mile out, and as he crossed the line he collapsed exhausted; Grant had retired with engine trouble, and Mortimer dropped out after his knee struck a wall when he cornered too tightly. Herron went on to take the win. He described it afterwards as the greatest moment of his life, and at the prize presentation that evening he was carried shoulder-high by Ulster enthusiasts. The audience of over 5,000 almost lifted the roof off the Villa Marina when the mayor of Douglas presented him with the magnificent Mercury trophy. In his speech of thanks he paid tribute to Williams and his record-breaking ride in the race. Williams for his part told the audience that in TT racing, the only thing which mattered was who crossed the line first.

In the four lap Lightweight 250cc TT on the following Saturday, 12 June, conditions were far from ideal, the previous day having been a wash out. Herron looked keyed up on the start line as he watched favourite Chas Mortimer and Tony Rutter start before him. When the flag dropped for him to start the machine fired instantly, leaving the rider that he was paired with, Alex George, some distance astern as he powered down Bray Hill. After 10 miles he led Mortimer by one second, but Charlie Williams who had started ten seconds behind, was closing fast. The Cheshire rider was confident that he could add to his tally on wins in what was becoming his most successful class. Williams remembered:

> I picked up my first signal board at Sulby and was shocked to see that I was in 2nd place just a couple of seconds down on Tom. I seem to remember that there had been some rain the previous night and consequently, there were some damp patches under the trees and it

was quite tricky. I rode as hard as I could but by the time I completed the opening lap, I was still second to Tom by just under two seconds. On the second lap I was trying harder than I perhaps wanted to and had a few moments on those damp patches. Still I was making no impression on Tom; in fact he was slowly building on his advantage.[13]

At 15 miles out Herron got a signal warning him of the threat, but Williams soon retired with a petrol leak which poured greasy two-stroke fuel on to his back tyre. He slid off and was forced to retire. He remembered afterwards:

When, back in our TT workshop we stripped the carbs and found small pieces of rubber in the bottom of the float bowls, it looked for all the world as if the petrol pipes had disintegrated internally, but on inspection they were intact. It was a mystery, and to this day, a mystery that has never been solved.[14]

A frantic pit stop followed for Herron, but the Japanese rider Takizuma Katayama was faster in his refuelling, and a real battle was now on. On the final lap, the flashing of scoreboard lights showed that the two were almost neck and neck. When Herron finally came into view, twenty-five seconds ahead of his rival, to take the chequered flag a tremendous cheer went up from the Grandstand. He told reporters that he had had an uneventful ride apart from one moment, when a damp patch caused a momentary skid. As well as setting a new race record for this class, the win on the Island put him into the lead in the 250cc World Championship that year, by one point from Walter Villa. This was the first time that an Ulsterman had led a World Championship since Ralph Bryans in 1965.

By winning the Senior and Lightweight (250) races on TZ 'C' Yamahas, Herron also became the first Irishman to win two TTs in one year since 'works' Moto Guzzi rider Stanley Woods in 1935. At the end of the year, Tom finished fourth in the 250cc World Championship behind Villa, Katayama and Bonera. Today Herron's Senior and Lightweight-winning Yamahas are lovingly preserved as part of the collection of Ulster racing aficionado Eddie Mateer.

In the Classic TT at the finale of race week, Yamaha mounted Alex George battled with John Williams for victory. The race was also held on the Saturday, because of the previous day's bad weather, and immediately followed the Lightweight TT. It was widely expected to be a Kawasaki/Suzuki grudge match, but a clutch of Yamahas also lined up on the grid, including those of Neil Tuxworth, and Tony Rutter with the machine that he had previously ridden to second place in the Junior, earlier in the week. Grant's powerful 750cc Kawasaki seemed a hot favourite until he reached Ballacraine, when gremlins put him out of contention, or so it seemed. After some fettling, Grant managed to restart and rejoined the race. At Ballaugh Bridge Suzuki-mounted John Williams was in the lead with a fifteen second advantage over Alex George and Charlie Williams. By the end of lap one his lead was twenty-one seconds, whilst behind Alex George with a 750cc Yamaha battled with Tony Rutter. Favourite Mick Grant was more than a minute adrift now, and when he finally went out with clutch trouble, there was no doubt that John Williams commanded the race, with Yamaha mounted challengers Rutter, Alex George and Charlie Williams crossing the line behind him. Williams' Suzuki had taken the win, but Yamaha machines filled the next nine of the top ten places. George, who finished second told *Manx Radio*'s Peter Kneale:

We had a little bit of brake bother on the last lap, apart from that it was all ok ... Apart from that it was very good; the 250 race was four laps, plus this was six laps so it's a lot of work, and I'm feeling a little tired, but other than that everything is OK. I'm very glad to finish.[15]

Third-placed rider Tony Rutter was also feeling weary after competing in the morning's Lightweight race, and added:

[I had] no problems whatsoever, a trouble free run. I ran out of petrol on the third lap, on the top of the Mountain, but I'd got a reserve tank and I switched that on, and a few seconds later it came back into life again. Actually I expected to have to turn the fuel on, but I'd forgotten all about it till it stopped![16]

The 1977 Junior TT was won by Charlie Williams; in conditions more like December than June the riders pushed off to start their long journey and it was scarcely any time before Charlie asserted his superiority over the rain lashed field. At Ballacraine, 6 miles out Williams led the field on the road and also on corrected time by six seconds from Scotsman, Bill Simpson with Tom Herron struggling in fifth place. Tony Rutter another of the favourites toured in at this stage and was obviously in trouble. At Ballaugh Bridge it was Williams again who flashed through first on the road and despite a bad leap over the famous hump back bridge he retained his advantage overall by two seconds from Simpson, with Herron fighting Ian Richards for third place. At Ramsey, Williams still showed the way retaining his lead of two seconds. Then to the mountain section and as the riders steamed through the Bungalow, Williams sent up a plume of spray as he held on grimly to the lead. He was now however only one second ahead of the relentless Simpson, with Herron trailing by eighteen seconds at this stage. Back to the Grandstand in Douglas and the crowd strained forward to catch their first glimpse of the riders. It was Williams who came through first then Simpson. Lap two saw Williams increase his lead to eleven seconds, and by the final lap he looked to have the race in the bag as he had twenty-three seconds in hand ahead of Simpson the next placed man. The road was so wet however that several riders slide off and others were just concentrating on stating upright and holding their place. Williams took the win, but the appalling weather ruined the race as a spectacle.

There was no Lightweight race in that year's TT, as in a shake-up of classes, the 350cc machines had become a subclass of the Senior and the 250s had taken their place. The 1977 Senior was won by the resurgent Phil Read, now Suzuki mounted, but in worsening weather conditions it was Ulsterman Tom Herron who finished second. Herron commented:

> It was a little bit hairy, the frame or the steering damper seemed to have given up and I was getting an awful lot of wobbles. On the first lap I thought it was the heavy fuel in the tank, and I said 'Oh it'll be ok, it'll get better,' it didn't it got worse and worse! I knew I had the easier machine for handling – normally. Today it was six of one and half a dozen of the other! It was just a problem with the frame, the engine was perfect.[17]

The 1977 Classic TT was billed as a two-way battle between the Kawasaki of Mick Grant, and the Suzuki of John Williams. Conditions were windy, which might have been expected to affect speeds, but despite going off on the slip road at Ballacraine,

Grant took command of the race. John Williams slipped off at Creg-ny-Baa, but Charlie Williams climbed through the field, and brought in a gaggle of Yamahas for second place. He remembered: 'I really enjoyed myself – much more than in Saturday's 250 race which I won. There was something to go at here, but I am slightly disappointed that I didn't lap faster than I did. My best lap was 109 and I had thought I could top 111.'[18]

Back at the Grandstand after the race he told Peter Kneale that the machine had begun to airlock on the descent from the Mountain, but quick action prevented the engine from stalling:

> I was not quite as quick as I anticipated actually, I had some problems, the steering damper broke on the third lap and I rode the last three and a half laps without a steering damper, which made it quite hairy in places, and also I had a problem with the petrol tank breather blocking up and the machine kept on cutting out, indeed going down through the Creg on the last lap when I came out, the crowds were waving and I waved back to them, and just as I put my hand back on the handlebars the whole bike cut out dead – I thought well its run out of petrol. I whipped the petrol tank cap open and then luckily it carried on again. It wasn't a brave thing to wave, I'm an idiot![19]

Third placed man Eddie Roberts, Beale Maxton Yamaha, who had diced with Chas Mortimer for much of the race, also had a few words to say:

> The collar bone is a bit sore, but then again when you see you're in the leader board positions you tend to forget

about the pain a bit. [Chas and I] were going round at pretty much the same speed, but when I got a few stones from his back wheel I decided that it was time to clear off.[20]

Birkenhead man Roberts had dabbled with Grand Prix racing on the Continent, but gradually became more focussed as a TT rider once he realised that he was unlikely to get a factory ride in the GPs. Roberts was also riding Yamaha machinery in the Jubilee race at the end of the week and told reporters from his local newspaper, the *Liverpool Echo* that although the Classic TT allowed for machinery up to 1,000cc, he had opted to use his 350cc machine: 'I've got a 750cc bike but I went for the 350cc because of the reliability rather than the speed.' He added that in the forthcoming Jubilee race, though the organisers also accepted engines up to 1,000cc he would probably be using his trusty 350cc Yamaha once again, saying: 'I am aiming for reliability again.'[21]

This one-off special event was introduced just for the 1977 TT schedule. The Schweppes Jubilee 1,000 TT, held to mark the twenty-fifth anniversary of the coronation of Queen Elizabeth II, was open only to those who had not previously won a TT. Victory was taken by an up and coming young rider from Ballymoney, Northern Ireland named Joey Dunlop, only a year after his TT debut. Arguably still the most famous name at the TT more than twenty years after his death, at this point Dunlop was still little known outside of Ulster racing circles. By now however, Joey had got his hands on an ex-Pat Mahoney 750cc Yamaha four, and as with his other machines quickly swapped the frame for a sturdier Seeley model, albeit one which was three years old and which had been intended for a Suzuki, hence its twin-shock configuration. The exhausts too were cobbled together, a rather crude copy of the crossover pipe layout on Tom Herron's latest TZ. Somehow or other Joey's mechanics managed to make it work. Special rules meant that slicks were not allowed and the race was to be run on treaded tyres. Joey topped the practice leader board with a speed of 106.80mph, thanks largely to some help from Tom Herron, who had been passing on tips and advice. Joey remembered afterwards: 'Before he dashed off to the Yugoslav GP Tom had shown me the way round and I learned an awful lot. There were bends I was struggling with but when he explained the lines I was even able to take them flat-out on my 750.'[22]

Despite the promising performance in practice, in the race itself the bike ran anything but smoothly, and it was at Braddan Bridge before all four cylinders were firing. Still he managed to put in a blistering first lap, and the threatened challenge from Eddie Roberts failed to materialise, but problems were looming. In practice the hard twin-shock suspension had wrecked a treaded tyre in two laps, but now it was expected to last for four. Worse still, the lockwire holding the home made exhaust in place came adrift, threatening Dunlop with the black flag from marshals. Dunlop had already pitted for fuel, but his brother Jim was concerned that he might decide to come in again and change the rear, because he was now all alone in the pit bay, his fellow crewman having gone off for a cigarette. He need not have worried, because by the last lap Joey had established such a commanding lead that as he approached Ramsey he actually had time to stop and make a quick visual inspection of its condition. He knew then that the tyre would go the distance and this gave Joey the confidence to really throw the bike into the fast swoops coming back over the Mountain for the final time. So fast was he in fact, that he came within twenty seconds of taking TT superhero Mick Grant's outright lap record. The race carried a £1,000 first prize, and it placed him as the third fastest TT rider after Grant and John Williams.

Whilst Dunlop's star was still very much in its ascendency at this point, another legend of the TT chose this particular moment to descend from the firmament and walk amongst the mortals once more. Mike Hailwood's return to the TT in 1978 is best remembered for his magical win in the Formula 1 race aboard the Sports Motorcycles Ducati, but at the time, this was very much a side-deal and most of the media attention was focussed upon his eye-catching tie up with Yamaha and Martini. This came about through his manager and mentor Ted Macauley's friendship with Rod Gould and Paul Butler, who worked for Yamaha's European arm in Amsterdam. Mike had an agreement to race a 500cc machine in the Senior race, a 250cc in the Junior and a 750cc in the finale of race week, the Open Classic event. It was the latter which caused him most concern initially; in his heyday as a factory rider in the 1960s, 500cc was the maximum permitted engine size. Mike was unsure that he could handle the extra power until he had a low key try-out in the 1977 Manx Grand Prix, ostensibly whilst making a documentary.

Yamaha had recognised that Hailwood's return to top level racing was a publicity opportunity that was too good to miss. They quickly agreed to supply Mike with whatever machinery and support he needed, but they would not pay him any money to race. In a letter from their European headquarters in Amsterdam, they offered Macauley the loan of either a TZ250 or TZ350, a TZ750, and a 500cc four-cylinder machine which had previously been used by Giacomo Agostini during the 1977 World Championship season. This came with the stipulation that whilst the other machines might be ridden at other meetings, the 500cc Grand Prix machine was for use at the TT only.

Fortunately the sponsorship from Martini-Rossi, one of the best known drinks manufacturers of the 1970s, allowed the team to recruit on a temporary basis Mike's former mechanic at Honda, Nobby Clarke, who was now with Yamaha and looking after American world champion Kenny Roberts' machines; Trevor Tilbury, the Yamaha 250cc expert, and Jerry Wood, workshop manager at Yamaha. The Japanese firm agreed to release them all from their other commitments for the TT fortnight.

Hailwood's return to front-line racing was media gold and there was a massive turnout for a press conference held by Martini in a hotel suite in London's Haymarket. Mike was his usual urbane self, calm, witty and above all modest and self-effacing as he answered questions from the world's media. The motorcycle racing scene was not normally associated with an aperitif like Martini, the fans were more typically beer drinkers, but Hailwood had such class and charisma that the tie-up worked well, from both perspectives. The machines were painted in a striking combination of Hailwood's racing colours of red, white and gold, and Martini's blue and black stripes. Mike would not have things all his own way however, and was acutely aware of the calibre of rider that he would face at the TT in 1978.

Among those riders was a revitalised Chas Mortimer, returning after a poor 1977 season in which he had left the TT empty handed. This year he was mounted on a 350cc Johnson and Hollinwood Yamaha for the Senior and Classic races, and for the Junior TT he had a 250cc machine supplied by Midlands businessman Sid Griffiths. He also had sponsorship from cigarette lighter company Sarome once again. He felt confident, and told reporters: 'Everything is working out much better this year. The sponsorship is good, I've two new bikes and my mechanic Lionel [Angel] and I get on well together.'[23]

In the Senior TT Hailwood's start was poor. He admitted that he was too relaxed after his win in the Formula 1 race earlier in the week, and was not in the right frame of mind. He remembered afterwards:

> I couldn't get the 500 started in the Senior. I think I was opening the throttle too wide and it just wouldn't light up. I thought the way I was going I was going to have to run all the way round the course. I seemed to be pushing for ages before it started. There's a knack to starting these things and I just don't have it. Talk about being embarrassed ... I knew everybody was looking at me and that made me worse.[24]

Despite the shaky getaway, coupled with new tyres and brakes that he needed to bed in, by the second lap he was in third place, and looked poised to challenge race leader Pat Hennen. Unfortunately he wasn't aware of this at the time, as his pit boards were not where he expected them to be. He decided to press on anyway, that was until disaster struck. In the Glen Helen sector he got into a couple of huge tank slappers and realised that something was wrong. An adjustable steering damper that Hailwood had fitted at the last minute had failed, and made the machine almost unrideable. He limped back to the pits, doing little more than 40mph. At first Nobby Clarke thought that there was nothing which could be done. However, he unscrewed the damper and managed to fix it by adding a washer. The stop had taken more than two minutes, and not even a rider of Hailwood's calibre could make that back up. Still he pressed on, when he could have been forgiven for retiring in the pits. His race was further hampered by clutch trouble, and he also ran out of petrol, due to an underfilled quick filler, but when he spluttered to a halt at the Bungalow he borrowed some from a motorist parked by the course in order to make it back. Unfortunately it was neat petrol rather than two-stroke mix so he could not allow the engine to get too hot, and coasted where he could, just using power on the hills. He finished in twenty-eighth place. Despite all this, he managed a fastest circuit in excess of 112mph, his fastest lap at the TT ever up until that point. Technically, refuelling at an unofficial location was a disqualification offence, but Hailwood received a replica for his efforts all the same. To say this race was a disappointment was an understatement, as when it was on song the 500cc bike went like rocket, and had he not encountered other problems Mike might well have finished second.

Later in the week came the Junior. As with the 500cc machine, Hailwood had experienced difficulty in starting the Yamaha, so Trevor Tilbury had adjusted the jetting to make it easier. He managed to get away in good order but was hampered by lack of practice as much as anything else. He had only managed two laps, and had fallen off on one of those, which did not improve his confidence. He remembered:

> By the time I got going, having looked around me at all those lightweight specialists, I settled down just to enjoy myself. And, to a great degree, I suppose I did. There was no real pressure on me, not like there was when I was out on the biggies, and after a lap or two I seemed to get the hang of the thing a bit more. Once I'd done that, and once I'd had a few of the chaps come by me, I got going some. Trevor had put together a nice motor, it must have been just about the quickest in the race and, in the end, I knocked up the second or third fastest lap of the race.[25]

What really did for Hailwood's chances in this race however was a blunder with the size of fuel tank. Because they were unfamiliar with current TT regulations, no one in the Martini Yamaha team had realised that they were allowed to run a larger size, meaning only one pit stop. Thus Mike was forced to stop twice for fuel, dramatically affecting his race time. None the less he managed twelfth place. The race was won by Chas Mortimer, closely followed by Charlie Williams. Charlie remembered that the race was delayed due to poor weather, and run over only five laps instead of the scheduled six:

> On his day the vastly experienced Mortimer was a hard man to beat and he pulled out an early advantage building up a lead that at one time was more than 50 seconds. By the end of the race, I had reduced that gap to around 30 seconds, probably due to the fact that Chas, having such a comfortable advantage, eased back a little.[26]

The big race of the week was Friday's Open Classic. The race had been billed as a confrontation between the old master, Mike, and the new pretender, current TT maestro Mick Grant aboard his all-conquering Kawasaki. Hailwood had had misgivings about the 750cc machine he was due to ride right from the beginning. Nevertheless he had forced himself to tame it, and was now psychologically ready to go:

> I really wanted to sign off the week with a big win. After the Formula One success, and the failures that followed, I'd set myself the Classic as the target. If I'd won it, or even if I'd done well and finished within sight of Mick, I am sure I would have retired from TT racing.[27]

He lined up on the start line that day alongside George Fogarty (father of World Superbike champion Carl) who was also aboard a Yamaha, albeit one prepared by the Manchester firm of Sports Motorcycles. As it transpired, the ferocious 750cc Yamaha clattered and died on the first lap, just as Mike was drawing level with Grant. It was a disappointment, not just for Mike, but also for the many fans looking forward to the greatest dice of the week, Hailwood versus Grant. Some of them had even come over just for the Friday race. Grant too was disappointed, remembering:

> I felt cheated when Mike went out. You know, the question you always ask yourself ... I wonder, could I have beaten him? Now I'll never know. After he had gone there was, I felt, nobody else to worry about. And it was the easiest money I've earned for a long time. But I'm sure he was just as disappointed as me. I know he would have set me up as a target; he knew I was good at the TT and, I'm certain, he was curious to see just how good I was. If I was better than him. But now its all so much conjecture. But for me the Classic was devalued right there and then, the second I found out he'd not made it. I know it would have been one hell of a race and, though I don't like talking figures, I'm sure it would have been in the 115s.[28]

Hailwood told reporters afterwards:

> As you know we'd had a lot of problems with the bike, a standard TZ750E Yamaha during practice. It twice gave trouble with seized pistons but after the second rebuild I did two laps on it during the final Saturday morning practise session and it seemed OK. Because of the problems

I thought seriously about riding the 1977 works 500cc Yamaha instead, but eventually I decided to use the 750 because I thought we had it sorted and the extra power, particularly the acceleration, would be useful.

I was pleased it was a clutch start because, as those who saw my getaway in the 500cc race know, I'm not too good at starting big two strokes, I haven't quite got the knack! But with the engine running I made a good start and zoomed away. I intended to have a go and enjoy myself – and for the best part of half a lap all went well. I understand I was tieing [sic] on time with Mick Grant at Ballacraine – and that we were already four seconds up on John Williams and ten seconds ahead of Phil Read and Joey Dunlop.

So although I didn't know it at the time, things were shaping up well. Then, all of a sudden my dreams were shattered. Somewhere around Kirk Michael the engine went onto three cylinders. At first I thought it might be a plug. So I decided to press on as fast as I could and change it at the pits. Of course, I knew as far as a place was concerned I'd had it. You only have to lose a couple of minutes and that's it as far as first, second or third are concerned. I felt pretty sick about the whole thing and I felt even worse when the engine blew at Glen Duff. Seems it wasn't just a plug, probably a piston had holed initially and then at Glen Duff had disintegrated completely.[29]

It was the Yamaha mechanics who felt the embarrassment most keenly, and as Hailwood and Macauley were drowning their sorrows in the hotel bar that night, they were working away on the post mortem, trying to discover what had gone wrong, Around midnight, Hailwood joined them in the garage.

Motorcycle engine parts were strewn around. Eventually the answer came to light: a broken crankshaft. Hailwood, mindful as always of giving value for money to his many fans, felt that he had underperformed. He vowed to come back in 1979, but that was to be the end of his association with Yamaha.

In 1979 the Junior TT was back up to six laps for the first time since 1970, and Charlie Williams dominated every one of them. It came after an inauspicious start to the season however – Williams had lost his regular place in the Honda Britain Endurance Racing team when they had withdrawn from this event the previous year, and now had no rides at all set up for the TT. He remembered: 'It was Tom Herron who said, "the best thing you can do is get yourself a 250", which Kangol helmets paid for, "and get the engine down to Harald Bartol in Austria and get it sorted." Which I did.' [30]

Confusingly, during this period the Junior was a 250cc race, but Williams broke both Agostini's eleven-year-old Junior lap record and Bill Ivy's 250cc record with a circuit at 106.83mph and also set a new race record for good measure. He took the lead from the start and produced a blistering second lap, but it was on the third time past the Grandstand that he wrote his name in the record books. At the half way mark, Williams led from Australian Jeff Sayle and Chas Mortimer who was third. Sayle diced for much of the race with another Sydneysider (and fellow Yamaha rider) Graeme McGregor. Amazingly this was the first time the two Aussies had ever faced each other in a race. Most of the riders came into the pits to refuel at this point, shuffling their positions but Williams held his lead throughout, even though his own pitstop was less than impressive – the Maxton Yamaha had to be tilted to swill pints of spilled fuel from the belly pan of the fairing. Ulster's Tommy Robb, back at the TT for the first time in six years, brought his Yamaha into the pits to change plugs at the end of the first lap. The three and a half minutes spent there cost him any chance of a position in the race, though he rejoined afterwards. By the end of lap four, Williams was easing off as he was in a commanding lead. Chas Mortimer was third, but by the final lap he had dropped to fourth, just missing out on a podium position. Williams had been confident of success in thus even before he arrived on the Isle of Man that year. He told reporters: 'Providing everything went according to plan I knew a win was on the cards. I thought about this race weeks ago and had felt very confident about the whole thing ... the bike ran perfectly all the way.'[31]

Williams had his hands full, because 1979's TZ250F was another improvement on an already successful formula. An 11kg weight reduction was achieved through further changes to the frame, despite the fact that the factory reverted back to welded steel engine mounting brackets rather than the alloy ones on the previous year's 'E' model. Other changes included a steeper rake and an alloy swingarm, and the bike featured a new exhaust and mounting system, an additional O-ring (from the previous single O-ring) in the header pipe, new conrod, wider intake port and minor carburettor modifications. The primary drive gear picked up two teeth to match the twenty-five on the 350, and the cylinder drain tube was altered. A dipstick was also introduced and the brake callipers became cast alloy units like those of the 750. Power remained the same as it had since the 'D' variant with 53bhp at 10,500rpm. A new fairing adorned the machine, which was pointed below the header pipes and which eliminated the old aluminium belly pan. A new fuel tank and seat unit appeared, and the clutch cover was reduced in size to a pressed aluminium piece surrounding just the rear of the clutch unit. (The previous models had utilised a cast aluminium unit completely covering the clutch.)

The grand finale of the 1979 TT was the Classic race, in which Alex George famously beat the resurgent Mike Hailwood into second place. However it is an often overlooked fact that this was also a red letter day for Yamaha machinery. For this event, Williams had removed the 250cc engine from his Maxton framed machine, and put in a TZ350 engine, which he had received on loan for that season's racing from Harald Bartol. He remembered:

> As I had a 'deal' with Mitsui, the UK Yamaha importers, we also changed the fairing for one that advertised the fact and proudly displayed their name. [In the race] I was making steady progress, but was quite alarmed when halfway round on the fifth lap, the dural plate which held the Krober rev counter on its top side and the two Krober transistor boxes on its underside fractured, leaving the whole kit and caboodle bouncing around under the screen.
>
> When, on Harald Bartol's advice I had fitted the Krober ignition system at the beginning of the season, the instructions stated that the two transistor boxes should not be fitted any closer than at least 10mm to any other object so as to isolate them from vibration. Now, these ultra delicate boxes, along with the rev counter were dancing around in the front of the fairing; the only barrier to stop them falling on to the front mudguard was the front fairing mounting tube.
>
> Surely it was a case of when, not if, the ignition would fail. I didn't help the situation as, when I emerged from the bumpier parts of the punishing TT course I couldn't read the rev counter, as it would fall out of my sight. So I would grab it firmly with my left hand and push the two rubber mounted boxes over the fairing mounting thus

enabling me, for a while at least, to get a look at it from time to time.

Incredibly, the bike never missed a beat! And I finished the race in third position having lapped at over 112mph, the fastest lap ever for a 350 up to that point.[32]

Williams regarded it as one of the best rides of his career, and to bring home a result like this on a 350cc engine against machines of up to 1,000cc was an incredible achievement.

In 1980, the opening event of race week was the Formula 1 race on the Monday, which was a slogging match between the big-engined Hondas and Suzukis. In the Senior on the Tuesday, Charlie Williams was confident of his chances aboard the Ted Broad-tuned Mitsui 500cc Yamaha four. At the end of practice week he told reporters: 'The speed is impressive. So too is the handling. Changing directions is easy and its good on slow bends. The gearbox is the only worry but a bearing has been inserted in the clutch which we hope will cure any problems.'[33]

In the event however the machine did not simply fail to go the distance, it barely got off the line. It was the Mitsui Yamaha team boss, Robert Jackson, who had said that it would be a good idea for Williams to ride team mate Dave Potter's TZ500 machine in this race. Charlie had practiced on it with good results. However when it came to the race it was rather a different matter, as he waited on the start line with Yamaha tuner and manager Ted Broad, who looked after Potter's machines on the short circuits. The problem was that Broad had no TT experience, and wasn't prepared for what could happen if two strokes were not kept bubbling. The race was due to start at eleven that morning, and in accordance with TT starting practice the bike had now been sitting idle for more than ten minutes; Charlie relates what happened next:

They had warmed the bike up before the race, and I could see the needle on the temperature gauge going down and down; now with my twins that wouldn't be a problem because I always had a thumb choke, so if it needed a little bit of choke you just dabbed it and you were away to go. With this thing, they had chokes but they were all just the little pull types, you had to twist them, but you couldn't even get to the bloody thing. They were just no good at all, so I was a bit worried about this. I said to Ted, 'You need to get some more heat in that bike.' He was all, 'Oh you'll be alright mate'. I should have insisted, and I didn't, so I pushed the bloody thing the whole length of the pits and eventually right to the top of Bray Hill. OK, I'd given up trying to start it, and by the bottom of the pits I was knackered, so I just thought I'd push it to the top of Bray Hill, what else could I do? And I just sort of flopped on it, went down Bray Hill and it fired up and think it had got that much fuel in there that it just caused it to hydraulic and bent a con rod, and it stopped at the Hawthorne.[34]

It was typical of the way a simple mischance happening could rob a rider of potential race victory. A little more heat in the engine, or a couple of cables connected to two of the four carbs might have meant another TT win for Williams, but it was not to be. He spent the rest of the race at the Hawthorne pub watching the front runners fight it out for Senior glory. The race became a Suzuki versus Suzuki battle, with the best-finishing Yamaha being that of Tony Rutter in fifth place.

Nevertheless, in the smaller categories, Yamaha was still strong. The 1980 Formula 2 TT gave Charlie Williams his eighth TT win, and marked a successful debut for the new water cooled LC350 Yamaha roadster. In fact, Williams was using the LD350 engine, in what was basically a TZ frame. As a result, a protest was lodged that the machine did not comply with the rules for this class in that 1,000 examples had not been sold to the general public before 31 March that year. Eventually the international jury threw out the protest on the grounds that it was both late and incorrect – 1,000 units had indeed been sold. In the race, Williams led from start to finish, his only worry was the Honda of Bill Smith. He told reporters afterwards: 'I was pleased when I caught Bill at Glen Helen on lap one. He came alongside at the end of the Cronk-y-Voddy straight. The Honda may have more top end but my Yamaha is better on acceleration.'[35]

The bike was prepared by John Gibbons from Burscough and Williams admitted that although it was not the fastest bike in the race, it was well set up for the tricky weather conditions on that particular occasion, and as well as the race win it gave him the fastest lap. Williams also had success in the 250cc Junior race, later the same day, riding the Team Mitsui Yamaha. This team was run by the British importers for Yamaha, and for the first time in almost a decade, Williams was back on standard factory frames, rather than Maxtons. He remembered that by this stage Yamaha's own frame had improved greatly so there was in fact now little to choose between them.

The 1980 TZ250 'G' model was a further departure from the norm of the past three or four years. New, larger diameter forks were fitted in an effort to combat the front end 'patter' problem which was frustrating so many riders. Motor-wise Yamaha went all-out for peak horsepower, at the expense of engine lifespan, by drastically increasing the inlet timing period. To do this they removed almost 8mm from the rear of the pistons (and thus also slightly increased the bore size).

This modification caused real problems with piston wear, despite the factory's attempt to counteract it with the inclusion of a short supporting 'tongue', protruding down from the top of the inlet port, in a vain attempt to reduce piston rocking. TZ250G's were, as a result, particularly expensive to maintain, requiring rebuilds after every race, though few riders complained about the extra 4bhp which it provided over the previous D/E/F models! Yamaha also increased the width of the secondary transfers slightly in this version, as well as fitting power jet carburettors.

Williams led from start to finish, but was forced into a dash for home on the last lap, when he was pressured by newcomer Donny Robinson, also Yamaha mounted. Before the race, Robinson had asked him where the wet patches were. 'You'll find them Donny!' was Williams' answer! As he passed Windy Corner for the last time in the four lap race (foreshortened by worsening weather) he saw a pit board which indicated that his previously unassailable lead had dropped to just six seconds, and he decided to take no chances. He opened the throttle wide from there until he crossed the finish line, taking first place with Robinson in second place.

The finale of the week however was a different story. Williams had a 750cc Mitsui machine entered for Friday's big race, the Classic, but retired on the opening lap. The race was billed as a showdown between the two then biggest names at the TT, Williams himself and Mick Grant. But it fell to another Yamaha, albeit one without factory support, to take the glory. In 1980 Joey Dunlop became the fastest rider in TT history when he won the Open Classic with an unbelievable lap record of 115.2mph, 9.2 seconds better than the old speed. Riding a Yamaha sponsored by John Rea from Templepatrick, Dunlop took on the might of the Japanese Honda firm and won hands down, but this was by no means a foregone conclusion. Although he was clearly a solid TT performer, Dunlop's last win was three seasons previously, and the total dominance that he would eventually achieve still lay some years into the future. For most of the race he had to battle with Honda team leader Mick Grant, and in fact the event developed on much the same lines as the previous year, when Honda's Alex George just edged out Yamaha's Mike Hailwood. Mick Grant remembered the race ruefully, as he had initially dismissed the 750cc machine – the same one on which Dunlop had taken victory in the Jubilee TT of 1977 – as a scruffy mess which would pose no serious threat to a factory team. He was in for a rude awakening, commenting:

> Joey's boys had bodged together the biggest fuel tank you've ever seen. It may have been ugly, but it held eight gallons and saved him a fuel stop – and the quickest fillers in existence can't beat that. Leaving Ballacraine for the last time, my signals said I was less than a second behind and I still thought I was in with a chance. But Joey's last lap was phenomenal – the first at 115mph – and he won by 20 seconds ... for years Joey described this as the most satisfying of all his TT wins, being 'tickled pink because he'd outwitted all the factory boys'.[36]

It was not all plain sailing for Dunlop however, as his mechanic Jacky Graham and his father William had worked on the bike all through the previous night. Joey himself had worked on it until 2.30am. He remembered:

> Throughout practice I had been having big trouble. I just couldn't get the big Yamaha to handle. Then at the very last moment, we noticed the rear wheel spacers were in back

to front. The 750 motor seemed to go OK. It was the same one that I rode in the Island two years before. This time, we had to stop only once for juice. I had an eight gallon tank fitted. It was a bit of a monster for a little guy like me, especially as I couldn't find a screen high enough to cover the tank and my helmet. At Bray on the first lap with all that weight on and still scrubbing in a new tyre – Dunlop of course! – I took things very gently. At Ballacraine on the first lap, two of the tank straps broke. I was really scared at Ballaugh Bridge because I thought at the hump back's leap the tank would come out of the frame and pull the petrol pipes off. I took it very gingerly there every lap – and even then I had one anxious landing. The tank got so bad on the first lap I thought I was going to have to retire as I approached Ramsey. Everywhere there were bumps I was taking it easy. At the refuelling stop, I took a mighty long time. Unlike some others, we didn't have a quick filler. But last year in the 250 I ran out of petrol on the last lap. Once bitten, twice shy. I wasn't leaving that pit till I knew the tank was completely full. There were going to be no mistakes this time – even if it did cost time.[37]

He was encouraged by the hundreds of Irish fans all around the course who were cheering themselves hoarse. Although he was leading, he couldn't work out who was second, and thought early on that Grant had retired. He expected the Honda rider to have been much closer on the road, and the first that he knew he was still in contention was in the pit lane when a commentator announced that Grant was arriving just as Dunlop was leaving. He knew that the lap record was within reach on his final circuit, with the weight in the tank now almost gone, the bike was running as smooth as a Bushmills whiskey, in Joey's own words.

The weather conditions were also ideal. In fact the only problem he encountered on his final lap was with a tear-off visor which stubbornly refused to detach, and which was rapidly becoming covered in flies. Amazingly, Dunlop had almost given up racing when his friend Mervyn Robinson was killed at the North West 200 a few weeks earlier, but now he was holding a cheque for £8,000, the biggest prize that he had ever won.

By 1981, Yamaha's decade long dominance in the solo races at the TT was a thing of the past. In the big bike classes, it had now become an all-out battle between a resurgent Honda, and a Suzuki-GB team with a serious point to prove. The 750cc class had now been dropped from the race schedule, ironically the TZ750 'Heavyweight Hurricane' came to dominate F750 racing around the world so completely that it caused its eventual demise (even though just 609 examples of the type were produced by Yamaha, in the model's 9 years of existence up to 1983) and of the 3 headline races of the week, the Classic, Formula 1 and the Senior, Yamaha managed a best result of only second place in the Senior, with Donny Robinson. The only Yamaha win came in the lowly Formula 3 class, with Barry Smith. Charlie Williams persevered with his Yamahas in the smaller classes, but had to be content with third places in the Junior and Formula 2 class. Williams nevertheless was at this time the most successful TT rider who was still racing, with nine victories to his name as well as holding the lap records in the 250 and 350cc classes. For Williams, the TT was still the highlight of his year, and he told journalists: 'Victory in the Island gives me the greatest sense of achievement. To me a TT win means more than a Grand Prix win.'[38] He went on:

> With the lighter bikes I feel that I can realise their full potential. I have had success on larger machines, but

I feel it is more a matter of getting round the corners and blasting down the straights. On the 250's and 350's you must be a really neat rider.[39]

But it was to be a bad week for him, as he struggled with an injured elbow in the 250cc TT and was in so much pain by the Wednesday that he almost did not start the Formula 2 race. To cap it all, a throttle clip broke whilst he rounded the thirty-third milestone on the Mountain. The throttle came away in his hand but he managed to finish the lap before retiring. However, if Yamaha efforts in the solo classes were now faltering, in the sidecar classes, it was a very different story. The suitability of TZ engines for three-wheeled racing had started to become evident in the early 1970s; they were reliable and strong, and importantly the spares were cheap and readily available. Now, at the beginning of a new decade they were reaching the peak of their dominance and were carrying all before them.

Chapter Five

1974–1981
SIDECAR SUCCESS

In the 1960s, the sidecar events at the TT had largely been dominated by German and Swiss riders on BMW engined outfits. However by the mid-1970s British drivers had begun a fightback, which was to a large extent due to the arrival of the Yamaha TZ750 engine. It was affordable, easily obtainable, reliable and worked well in a sidecar outfit. Among the first of the British sidecar drivers to adopt the Yamaha was Mac Hobson, who managed fourth place in the 1974 500cc race. He was followed by a slew of other riders the following year, and this time he managed a second place in the 500cc race, matched by Dick Greasley in the 1,000cc event. In 1976 Hobson won the 1,000cc race, and by this time about half of the entries were Yamaha mounted. The man who would take this engine, together with a Windle chassis, into the TT history books was George O'Dell, when in 1977 together with passenger Kenny Arthur he broke the 100mph barrier for sidecars in the Isle of Man, in the same year that he secured the Sidecar World Championship. It was one of the most memorable events in sidecar history and O'Dell, though his TT career was short, was one of the most colourful characters that the sport has produced. The story of the battle for the ton in the sidecar TT is one of the most dramatic episodes to come from the Isle of Man's Mountain Course.

George O'Dell was born in Hemel Hempstead in 1945, and worked as an engineer at Kents Brushworks. He had been a leather-clad rocker in his youth, until an accident on his road bike lessened his interest in two-wheelers, and instead he begin to consider three. O'Dell's involvement in sidecar racing quickly grew. He made his Isle of Man debut in 1970, but the 1971 TT was almost his last, when a bad crash put both O'Dell and his passenger in hospital. Many of his early rides were on BSA machinery, before converting to König two-stroke technology like a number of his contemporaries. O'Dell's fiery character made him determined to make his mark on the Grand Prix scene, and in 1975 his attitude made an impression on Eric May, a Berkshire businessman who became a major sponsor. It was May who purchased for O'Dell his first TZ engine, acquired through a Swiss Yamaha importer.

Having the Yamaha engine alone however was not enough to bring success. O'Dell used it with a chassis made by one of the greatest constructors in British sidecar history, Terry Windle. A machinist by trade, Windle started racing solos in 1961, with his first race being at Rhydymwyn in Wales. His solo career was short lived however, as he soon took up sidecar racing. This led to him building his own chassis in his garage before opening up his own workshop in the village of Thurgoland. His sidecar chassis building career spanned over forty years, and even after officially retiring in 2008 he continued to build bikes again in the garage behind his house. Through this time his chassis won five World Championships with riders George O'Dell, Jock Taylor, Darren Dixon and twice with Steve Abbott. O'Dell began using the Windle outfit almost by accident. He had sold his previous machine in 1975 and had intended to build his own hub-centred steering outfit. However, he did not complete it in time for the 1976 season, and so purchased the Windle as a stop gap. Although unintended, it was a good move – as O'Dell later commented, Windle machinery was ideally suited for the bumpy TT circuit. However 1976 was not a great year for O'Dell at the TT. His regular passenger was badly injured in a collision with a wall, and he returned home from the event with nothing. At the same time however he was making progress and gaining experience in Grand Prix events in Europe, and acquired a new passenger in the form of Kenny Arthur, a maintenance engineer with Lever Brothers on Merseyside. For the 1977 season O'Dell put all he had into the purchase of a Seymaz chassis, which would be his main outfit. However the trusty Windle remained his back up, and with the Seymaz damaged at Cadwell Park in the spring of 1977, it was to take centre stage at that year's TT. Unlike the previous year, in which it had appeared in the yellow and green livery of main sponsor BP, this time it was in the distinctive yellow and red of Shell. So highly was O'Dell regarded by this stage, that the rival oil company had made him a financial offer which he simply could not refuse. Passenger Kenny Arthur remembered:

> The Windle was a very stable bike particularly around the Isle of Man. It was well-proven ... Lots of people had used them and you felt very confident on the bike. It was one of those bikes you could change direction on it and not feel endangered in any way – and nicely put together, it was really well engineered. Compared to the bikes today I don't suppose it was, but it just felt right. It felt very right. The circuit was a lot bumpier then, and some of the corners were a lot tighter, but the bike was good ... It was a four cylinder two stroke Yamaha, 750cc, which was the same engine that we used for Grands Prix, only you put 250 cylinders and pistons and exhausts on it, which took

it down to a 500 for Grands Prix. Grands Prix were always 500cc at that particular time, and internationals were 750 or 700 depending on what cylinders you used. But it was a lovely bike, very kind, very reliable. And George did the engine, I never touched the engine at all. We had one mechanic who came with us to do the chassis, which I was quite capable of doing, but they did it down south and so they were more familiar with it than I was, and I wasn't so much hands on at that particular time with the mechanicing for George because the bike was pretty much ready, I think it was everything else that wasn't ready, the bike was always done first![1]

O'Dell went to the 1977 TT in the midst of his campaign for the World Championship title that year. Although this was the first time that a TT win would carry no points towards that title, the two sidecar races on the Isle of Man were still eagerly anticipated, and certain to be hotly contested. The first practice session on the Island demonstrated just how severely an outfit could be battered by the bumpy roads – the Windle came back in to the pits with a main chassis tube broken, a loose rear sprocket, and a crack to a rear suspension mount. It took an all-night session in a rented garage in Douglas to put the damage right, but the outfit was ready for the second sidecar practice, run the following afternoon. O'Dell and the mechanics also made a series of modifications, including going up a jet size on the carburettor to 310 instead of 300 used on the UK circuits, in order to give more power on the climb up the mountain. They had also used a harder spark plug, an N82G, in order to prevent it melting with the heat and possibly dropping into the cylinder, and opted to put a size nineteen sprocket (the largest) on the engine with the smallest possible (a thirty-three) on the rear wheel. When it was airborne, the engine would rev to an additional 1,000rpm before the back wheel bit into the road again, pulling the engine back with enormous force as it did so. All of that force was transferred through the chain, and at the Isle of Man TT a chain could stretch by as much as the length of a link over several laps. To help cope with this the chain manufacturer Renold had supplied O'Dell with a new experimental version made of harder steel, which reduced stretching considerably. There was nothing experimental or revolutionary about his tyres however, they were standard Goodyear G50 slicks. His radiator was one from a cannibalised Suzuki road bike, fitted because it was considerably lighter than the Yamaha equivalent, and at a slight angle in order to minimise the damage caused by stones flicked out from the rear wheel of an outfit in front.

The magical 100mph sidecar lap had almost been achieved in 1976, when Yamaha-powered Mac Hobson and Mick Burns had lapped at 99.962mph. Now there was much speculation as to whether 1977 would see the barrier broken. With the bike back in good order and with his familiarity with the Mountain Circuit returning after a year away, O'Dell felt confident enough to push things as hard as he could during the second practice. After the first two laps O'Dell pulled into the pits to check that everything was still in place on the bike, and to make sure that his passenger Kenny Arthur was comfortable with the performance so far. On the third lap, from a standing start O'Dell launched the pairing into the history books, achieving an incredible 101.30mph. O'Dell remembered:

> It wasn't hard. There wasn't too much traffic out at the time, and any sidecars I did meet I seemed to catch at the best places to overtake without any trouble. There were a

few corners that I went through very quickly, at a speed I didn't think a sidecar could go through. Quarry Bends we sailed through just like greased lightening. At Cronk Y Voddy and Sulby, I went through fairly gently because those straights are so bumpy. I got a bit of elevation at Ballaugh Bridge which I normally do through failing to brake early enough. Over the Mountain I seemed to flash past the 32nd and 33rd milestones. Always have liked the Mountain section. But there were no problems at all. Didn't even get near any kerbs or grass.[2]

He continued with his description of the record breaking circuit:

Everything went so smoothly. I thought it was a good lap on the descent from the Mountain, coming down from Kate's Cottage to the Creg. The rest of the way home I knew there was only one place where there might be a hold up – Governor's Bridge. But there was only one bloke to pass after Governor's. Had we caught him going into Governor's he might have cost us 20 seconds which would have killed the lap. I'd watched Kenny out of the corner of my eye, flashing around, and I could tell he was enjoying himself. As I braked hard for Governor's the smell of burning brakes told me it must be a fast lap. I took it through the gears to 10,500 rpm as I screwed it over the line. You can waste five seconds by rolling it off at the finish. I overshot the gate to the paddock and we had to wheel it backwards.[3]

For Kenny Arthur as well there was an instinctive feeling that this lap was 'the one'. He remembered:

It didn't feel a lot different or a lot harder, [but] it was obvious that the bike was very quick in a straight line, and at the Isle of Man that's quite critical, because you knew by the bumps and the bangs that you were getting going round various places [it] was a lot quicker than you had ever been before, so it was pretty obvious that we were very close; there and thereabouts for doing the 100 mile an hour. I'd been very close once before so I had a good idea what it was going to be like, and it was good, it was OK ... I felt very confident, I never felt in trouble with George at any state in my racing career ever, he would alway seem to be in control, so I didn't have any qualms or questions, I just got on with the job ... When we got back we were quite shocked really. As soon as we rolled up in the paddock the boss of the Beresford [Hotel], John, he had a bottle of champagne, they were all standing there cheering and shouting, they said 'you've done it, you've done it.' So, OK it was in practice, but it was done, and when we got back to the hotel they'd painted all the windows ... It felt really good, really special. You don't realise until later in your life how special that moment was, its all in an adrenaline rush and 'of the moment.' After the moment you realise what a part of TT history that was.[4]

A record lap in practice is always considered to be 'unofficial' but for O'Dell that day it made no difference. When the timing officials showed him the pink slip with his time noted on it he knew that he had achieved a personal ambition which he had been chasing since his crash at the TT in 1971. Since then, O'Dell's respect for the circuit had only increased but at the same time, so had his determination to conquer it. At the time he learned of his achievement there were tears in his eyes, and that night he returned to the race office to stare at the practice leaderboard notice in the window, unable to take his eyes off his timing, before returning to the team lodgings at the Beresford Hotel where a party in his honour was in full swing.

For the first sidecar race of that 1977 TT O'Dell had been allocated the number sixteen, which greatly annoyed him. By rights he should have been in the top handful, but with a number as high as that he would have perhaps six crews to pass on the road before having a clear track in front of him, severely limiting his prospects in the race. His protests to the ACU fell on deaf ears however and there was nothing for it but for driver and passenger to equip themselves with a number of tear-off visors; there was a distinct possibility that they might get stuck behind another outfit blowing out oil mist and be unable to pass them for several miles. His chief opposition came in the form of Dick Greasley, with passenger Mick Skeels, and West German driver Rolf Steinhausen with passenger Wolfgang Kalauch. It was a four lap race with a pit stop, and for the first two as predicted O'Dell encountered heavy traffic on the road, which caused him to lose concentration and also affected his speed. When he pitted, things got worse with first a jammed fuel filler nozzle and then fuel accidentally spilled all over the passenger platform which had to be cleaned up if Kenny Arthur was to have any chance of staying onboard. The fuel was two-stroke mixture and Kenny remembered:

> It got a bit slippy, because there was oil in it and unfortunately we couldn't wipe it up. It was what they called a 'splash and dash' – it was a gallon in and then push off and you're ready to go. The other thing is, with a hot two stroke engine, they really take a lot of pushing,

and when you've just done two laps it's hard going. We pushed and pushed and then it fired up and we were gone, so it was good. It was a little bit slippy under foot, but I just managed to keep hold of the handles, I think that was important because it got on my leathers and on my knees, and with it having oil in the petrol I was sliding about a bit.[5]

However even being told that Greasley had already lapped at over 100mph did not phase O'Dell; if anything it made him more determined, and on the next lap he settled into the job in hand. On the third lap he overhauled Steinhausen, and at Ballaugh a board told him he had a lead of two seconds over Greasley. By the final lap that was up to forty seconds and eventually, although he never managed to pass him or even catch him on the road, O'Dell took the race from Greasley by fifty seconds. In the process he had pushed up the sidecar lap record to 102.80mph. He remembered:

The crowd made me do 102.80 mph. As I was catching different guys, people could see me coming and would wave like mad at these other drivers, telling them to move over. It was incredible. During the last lap I was lapping the late starters and, at Ramsey, the crowd went wild as they urged two slower outfits to let me through. Talk about being switched on. The Island was being great to me and everything was going as smooth as silk. On the last lap ... I experienced one of my best feelings in racing. The spectators were urging me on, everyone seemed to be waving. At the Gooseneck where you're going slowly, you're almost in personal contact with the crowd who are just a few feet away. I could tell they were with me.

They wanted me to catch Dick on the road – they knew he wasn't far ahead of me. Going through Brandish and Hillberry I thought some of them were going to get on my bike. They were going crazy and at Governor's I could hear them shouting.[6]

Everyone in the pits was elated, John Thompson from the Beresford Hotel had a Rolls Royce waiting with champagne and took the team back to the hotel where more supporters were eager to greet the two and to congratulate them on their achievement. The Windle outfit was battered on its return to the pits – the engine was worn out and had to be replaced before the next race, and a number of cracks to the chassis had to be welded. Kenny Arthur too had taken a buffeting and had to visit an osteopath for treatment to his back before the second race. Even Greasley, who always felt that he had the better claim to be the one who achieved the first 100mph sidecar lap, had a grudging respect for O'Dell and his performance that day. Many years later he wrote on his website:

> In 1977 ... I had kicked off the season with a new Windle outfit with wider wheels for more rubber on the road (or grass... delete accordingly!) and Mick Skeels took on the role of ballast. Although the chassis didn't handle as well as the previous sidecar, Mick and I got on well and immediately gelled putting in some solid performances. In our first TT together, there was great pressure as our main rivals had now also gone the 2 stroke route with Yamaha's, Barton's or Konig adapted marine engines. I had also been given number 2 which meant I was the hare being hounded by those in my wake! From the onset, I gave all I could. Throughout practising I had been getting

close to the 100mph lap, but I was surprised to achieve the first official ton sidecar lap on the mountain circuit and, certainly, from the standing start. George o' Dell has often been given the credit for it, but as he was following me, he wasn't the first over the line. But George was also flying that week and I have to say, he was exceptional in that race. His strength in some areas of the course were outstanding and he overtook me on the second lap and went on to win and completing the first ever 100mph average sidecar race.[7]

Race two was set to be another trailblazer and O'Dell was leading on time when the smell of burning clutch alerted him to possible problems. At Ballaugh the engine gave up the ghost, and he and Arthur spent the rest of the race in the Raven pub. O'Dell's main concern was that someone else would take his lap record, but he need not have worried. Even greater glory was to come for the Windle Yamaha later that year in the British Sidecar Grand Prix at Silverstone. O'Dell's other machine, a Seymaz, proved itself unreliable and so it was aboard his TT winning outfit that he clinched the necessary points to secure the 1977 Sidecar World Championship, the first British competitor to do so for twenty-four years. Amazingly, O'Dell's championship came without him ever having won a race, so consistent was he in securing podium positions, and it was a strange irony that the only race which he did win that year – the Isle of Man TT – no longer counted towards a world title.

The first sidecar race of 1978 saw one of the blackest days in three wheeled history on the Isle of Man. The race was only minutes old by the time three men lay dead; Mac Hobson, the man who had done so much to pioneer the use of Yamaha engines in sidecar outfits, and his passenger Kenny Birch died in a smash at the top of Bray Hill a few hundred yards from the start line, whilst in a separate incident at the bottom of the hill Swiss rider Ernst Trachsel was killed after colliding with the debris, whilst his passenger escaped with a broken leg. The race went on, but such tragedy eclipsed the success of Rolf Biland in setting a new lap record before retiring shortly ahead of finishing. Mac Hobson from Gosforth was a hugely popular character, and one of the biggest names in the North East Motorcycle Racing Club. He was leading the British sidecar champions at the time, and was lying in second place in the World Championships that year; the world series finished with him credited in fifth place posthumously. Knowing that Biland was faster, Hobson had planned to beat him to Quarter Bridge, but whilst overtaking his 750cc four-cylinder machine had struck a raised manhole cover off the racing line. Tragically the fact that there was a problem with this manhole cover following roadworks the previous winter was known, and it had been the subject of discussions between race organisers and representatives of the sidecar drivers the day before. The manhole was later removed, and 1978 was to be the last year that sidecars were set off from the line in pairs. The second race that year was taken by Steinhausen, with the up and coming talent of Mick Boddice in second place. Victory over the two legs went to another rising star, a young Scot named Jock Taylor.

John Robert 'Jock' Taylor was born in Pencaitland, near Edinburgh, and began racing in 1974 aged 19, as a sidecar passenger. By 1975 he was in the driving position, with an ex-Mac Hobson BSA twin. Like many other British champions he earned his spurs the hard way, struggling in his early club events with no financial backing. In those early years, he made do with worn tyres, tired engines and race fuel that was in short supply. One observer remembered that in his early days he would travel down to North Gloucester club meetings at Gaydon in Warwickshire. He used an old bus as a transporter and when it arrived at the trackside, out would pour a whole gang of faithful Scottish supporters. So loyal were these early fans that they even clubbed together to pay for the petrol to enable Taylor to get down to the meeting.

By 1977, Taylor had switched to Yamaha machinery and was starting to make a mark at British level, his most significant achievement up to that time being the setting of a new lap record of over 105mph at the Ulster Grand Prix. In the same year he won the Scottish Championship and came second in the British Championship with fellow Scot Lewis Ward in the chair. Together the two scored an eye-catching win at Oulton Park in Cheshire, and this brought Taylor to the attention of a major sponsor in the form of Fowlers of Bristol, one of the biggest motorcycle dealers in south-west England. In the 1978 season they backed him for a first attempt at the World Championship series. Despite Ward quitting mid-way through the year, with Fowlers' support Taylor put together a very creditable first season, with a third place in his home event, the British Grand Prix, fourth place in Czechoslovakia, sixth in Belgium, seventh in France and eighth in Italy, giving him an overall finish of seventh place.

The highlight of the 1978 season however was the Isle of Man TT, where with Kenny Arthur in the chair Jock finished second and third in the two sidecar legs, setting a new lap record of 101.22mph in the process. It was to be in 1979 that a winning pairing was born when, finding himself without a passenger for the Snetterton Race of Aces event, he appealed over the circuit tannoy for someone to come forward. From out of the solo paddock came a young Swede who had so far enjoyed only modest success – 22-year-old Bengt-Goran (Benga) Johansson.

After completing his two years of national service in the Swedish Army, Johansson (who was the son of a stock car racer from Ljungby near Anderstorp) rode a Morbidelli to second place in the Swedish Championship, but struggled to break into the Grand Prix circuit and sold the machine. Having tried his luck at UK meetings he had again achieved only patchy success. His interest in sidecars was slight until that day when he answered Taylor's appeal, but the two clicked right away and became a pairing for the remainder of Taylor's career. With Johansson on board he took his maiden Grand Prix win just a few weeks after meeting him for the first time, appropriately enough in front of the passenger's home fans in Sweden. Up to that point, Taylor had been using a hub-centred Seymaz chassis, but later that year he acquired from Terry Windle a short wheelbase outfit. It was on this machine that Taylor would enjoy so much success, both on and off the Isle of Man.

By 1980 the Scottish/Swedish pairing were poised for an all-out assault on the world title. Fowlers' racing boss, renowned engine builder Dennis Trollope, had put together no less than fifteen 500cc Yamaha engines on which to carry the world campaign, along with a further selection of 750cc motors for use in international meetings like the Isle of Man TT. With other financial backing in place as well, this meant that all Taylor had to supply was his riding talent. He took victory at the Dutch TT, and the Belgian and Finnish Grands Prix, so that by the time he reached the British Grand Prix at Silverstone in August that year, the title was within his reach. Despite two of his main rivals dropping out with mechanical troubles, the race was still full of drama, with Taylor and Johansson suffering a slow puncture which cost them first place. Finishing second however was enough to hand them the 1980 world title. The same season had witnessed them raise the bar again at the TT, on the Windle chassis. Johansson had only seen the TT course for the first time in January of that year, and after an intense return visit in May in which he crammed in fifteen laps in a car, he felt that he knew the layout sufficiently well. In practice week his course knowledge grew further and he began to feel more and more comfortable with the Mountain Circuit. His only difficulties, he recalled later, came from the bumpy surface (despite having fitted extra padding to the sidecar platform in order to try to compensate) and from the glare of the setting sun during evening practice sessions. After battling to second place in wet conditions during the first race, they won the Sidecar B event convincingly and chopped twenty-eight seconds off the lap record in the process, taking it now to 106.08mph.

In 1981 Taylor retained his British title and claimed further laurels in the TT, taking his tally of wins there to three. After wearing out two engines during practice week, they went into the first race with a brand new 700cc engine built just the night before by Dennis Trollope. Described by *Motorcycle News* as 'the world's most exciting sidecar partnership,' the two set off at a blistering pace and took an astonishing 24.2 seconds off their record lap time from the previous year. Johansson added afterwards: 'Coming from the GPs, it was completely different. There was no scratching at all. It was damp in Ramsey so we had to go carefully. I thought we'd do 103 or 105. I was really surprised we went round at 108 mph.'[8]

It was a close-run thing however as they finished the race with only fumes in the fuel tank, with Taylor explaining afterwards: 'We'd planned to stop for one or two gallons. But when it started to rain around Black Hut on the Mountain on the second lap I decided the extra petrol would be unnecessary.'[9]

As the tail enders completed their last lap, it developed into a real cloudburst but it was too late to really slow the leaders down. In the second sidecar event that year, the winners from Race A really showed how far ahead of the rest of the field they were. In spite of mechanical problems, which meant their speed was considerably down on the first outing, they still beat second place man Dick Greasley by nearly two minutes. They had started off slowly in order to try to preserve the Yamaha motor, and were hoping to complete the three laps without stopping for fuel. Only if they had been seriously pressed and forced to thrash the engine would they have to come into the pits. At first they were trailing main rival Trevor Ireson. However after Ballaugh Bridge they were in the lead by five seconds, even though they had experienced a major slide at the thirteenth milestone, after which Taylor slackened off again. The real drama however began on the mountain climb on the second lap when the fuel pump gave out, and they had to hand pump petrol to the engine. Yet it was still a commanding victory.

It was 1982 which was to see Taylor and Johansson's greatest achievement at the Isle of Man TT. It was however a disappointing story in the first sidecar race when, despite being favorites, the duo hit big problems on the first lap. Taylor was distracted by the temperature gauge, and they clipped a bank. They eventually finished eighteenth, whilst Mick Boddice who led for two laps, was forced to retire on the final lap with engine failure. Trevor Ireson (with passenger Donnie Williams) moved to the top of the leader board and had no such worries, taking the chequered flag in front of Greasley and Hanks.

Boddice's bad luck continued in the second race, which took place in glorious conditions. He led Taylor by a fraction of a second when he was forced out at Sulby Crossroads on the second lap. Taylor was cruising initially, as he needed to run in his Yamaha engine following an all-night repair job to fix a broken cylinder head stud, but turned up the wick to put himself four seconds ahead at the half-way point. With the departure of Boddice, Taylor took over control of the race, and even though he stopped for fuel at the end of lap two he still managed to shave two seconds off his lap record from the previous year. In the final blistering circuit he increased the lap record to 108.29mph, to win from husband and wife team Dennis and Julia Bingham, and Steve Abbott with Shaun Smith in third. Overall victory from the two races went to Roy Hanks and Vince Biggs, who were fifth in that second race, but Taylor's lap record was an astonishing achievement. Some measure of this can be gained from the fact that it stood unbroken for seven years. Indeed, there were some who said it would never be broken, and as the years rolled on, changes to the course (particularly to smooth out Sulby Straight, which at that time was like riding on corrugated iron, and to Quarry Bends which after road alterations became a gear faster) meant that it never could be beaten. Taylor himself put his astonishing speed down to the fact that this time round he had moved the temperature gauge, so that it was now Johansson's responsibility to watch it!

Just weeks after their achievement in the TT, Taylor and Johansson travelled to take part in the Finnish Grand Prix. Taylor had been developing a long wheelbase machine to compete in World Championships, and although he did not like the outfit due to its unfortunate tendency to leap across the road, he had decided to persevere with it. The more reliable four times TT winning short wheelbase machine was left at home, prepared in readiness for the forthcoming British Championship round at Donington. On race day at the Finnish circuit at Imatra, like the TT also a closed roads course, the heavens opened. Jock was the sidecar riders' representative and gave the go ahead for the Sidecar Grand Prix to take place. It was a decision to have fateful consequences. In the rain-soaked conditions, Taylor and Johansson's outfit aquaplaned and slid off at a corner, colliding with a telegraph pole as it did so. Taylor survived the initial impact, but as he was receiving attention from marshals at the scene another machine (piloted by a Finnish rider) suffered a similar misfortune and slid off at the same place. It collided with the wreckage of Taylor's outfit and the race was red flagged as medics attended the injured. Jock died that evening from the injuries sustained in the second crash. For his family and friends, the news was made all the more shocking by the fact that they learned of Jock's death via a BBC sport broadcast that night. Even today, more than thirty years after his death, many TT fans and competitors alike regard Jock Taylor as the greatest ever sidecar racer.

EPILOGUE

When Yamaha arrived at the TT in 1961 they were very much the underdogs, with main rivals Honda some two years ahead of them. But no one could fail to be impressed by the speed with which their technology improved. They quickly caught up with, and even surpassed, the all-conquering Hondas. In the hands of able and determined riders like Phil Read and Bill Ivy, they were formidable, even at times unbeatable. Soon their lightweight machines, which were fast and affordable, would become the dominant make on the Isle of Man. They won every 250cc Lightweight or Junior TT between 1970 and 1980, and whilst it might be argued that they never succeeded in achieving the same level of domination in the larger classes, the Yamaha name remains synonymous with two-stroke power. Throughout the 1970s their machines brought success to countless British and other riders, and it might be argued that what Honda started, in terms of the downfall of the British motorcycle industry, Yamaha completed.

The sheer versatility of their engines, in particular the TZ series, was also remarkable. They were powerful and reliable enough not just to be effective in solo racing, but also to carry two competitors in sidecar racing. It is no exaggeration to say that the greatest achievements of the 1970s in sidecar racing at the Isle of Man TT were by and large achieved on Yamaha machinery, and they attained the same level of dominance in that decade as BMW had achieved in the 1960s.

For many TT fans the sharp staccato dog-bark engine note, and the plume of blue smoke from the two-stroke engine are the colophon of these decades. Indeed so great did their dominance become that they drove four stroke engines out of racing almost entirely until the later 1980s. So ubiquitous was the Yamaha TZ engine on the Isle of Man that it has won more TT races than any other type of motor; indeed probably more than all other types combined.

NOTES

Introduction

1. Ted Macauley, *The Yamaha Legend*, New York, 1979, p.5
2. Macauley, p.14
3. Macauley, p.21

Chapter One: Turning the Tide, 1961–1965

1. *Classic Racer,* Number 204, July/August 2020, p.25
2. *Sound Stories 1963 TT,* Stanley Schofield Productions, author's transcript
3. Macauley, p.38
4. Macauley, *op cit*
5. Michelle Duff, *The Mike Duff Story: Make Haste Slowly,* Toronto, 1999, p.169
6. *Sound Stories 1964 TT,* Stanley Schofield Productions, author's transcript
7. Tommy Robb, *TT to Tokyo,* Douglas, 1974, p.88
8. Macauley, p.60
9. Duff, p.232
10. Alan Peck, *No Time to Lose – The Fast Moving World of Bill Ivy,* London, 1972, p.55
11. *Sound Stories 1965 TT,* Stanley Schofield Productions, author's transcript
12. *Op cit*
13. *Op cit*

Chapter Two: Who Wears the Crown? 1966–1968

1. *Sound Stories 1966 TT*, Stanley Schofield Productions, author's transcript
2. *Op cit*
3. *Op cit*
4. Peck, p.75
5. Luigi Taveri, *Mein Leben auf Zwei Rädern*, Stuttgart, 1969, p.210, author's translation
6. *Sound Stories 1967 TT*, Stanley Schofield Productions, author's transcript
7. *Sound Stories 1968 TT*, Stanley Schofield Productions, author's transcript
8. *Op cit*
9. *Motorcycle News*, 12 June 1968
10. *Op cit*
11. *Op cit*
12. *Sound Stories 1968 TT*, Stanley Schofield Productions, author's transcript

Chapter Three: The Age of the Privateer, 1969–1973

1. *Classic Bike Guide*, 20 April 2020
2. *Motor Cycle News*, 17 June 1970
3. https://www.youtube.com/watch?v=9ouD3X1CqFw, author's transcript
4. Charlie Williams, *It Was the Best of Times*, NL, 2019, p.43
5. Phil Read, *Rebel Read: The Prince of Speed*, Malta, 2014, p.158
6. Mick Grant, *Takin' the Mick*, Yeovil, 2012, p.92
7. *Motor Cycle News*, 16 June 1971
8. Macauley, p.85
9. *Motor Cycle News*, 14 June 1972
10. Stuart Barker, *Tourist Trophy Century*, London, 2007, p.168
11. *Motor Cycle News*, 14 June 1972
12. *Cycle World*, 15 June 1973

13. Robb, p.115
14. Robb, p.116
15. Charlie Williams, conversation with author
16. *Motor Cycle Mechanics*, September 1973, p.56
17. *Motor Cycle Mechanics*, September 1973, p.57
18. *Op cit*
19. *Classic Motorcycle Mechanics*, 25 November 2013

Chapter Four: The TZ Years, 1974–1981

1. Charlie Williams, conversation with author
2. *Motor Cycle News*, 5 June 1974
3. Grant, p.110
4. Williams, p.81
5. *Motor Cycle News*, 12 June 1974
6. *Motor Cycle News*, 28 May 1975
7. Williams, p.101
8. *Motorcycle Racing*, June 1978
9. *Motor Cycle News*, 11 June 1975
10. *Classic Racer*, March/April 2020, p.59
11. *Motorcycle Racing*, June 1978
12. *Motor Cycle News*, 9 June 1976
13. Williams, p.109
14. Williams, p.110
15. *The Story of the 1976 Isle of Man TT Races*, Sound News Productions, author's transcript
16. *Op cit*
17. *The Story of the 1977 Isle of Man TT Races*, Sound News Productions, author's transcript
18. *Motor Cycle News*, 22 June 1977
19. *The Story of the 1977 Isle of Man TT Races*, Sound News Productions, author's transcript
20. *Op cit*
21. *Liverpool Echo*, 17 June 1977

22. Mac McDiarmid, *Joey Dunlop: His Authorised Biography*, Yeovil, 2001, p.49
23. *Motorcycle Racing*, June 1978
24. Ted Macauley, *Mike the Bike – Again*, Dorchester, 2018, p.83
25. Macauley, p.84
26. Williams, p.141
27. Macauley, p.84
28. *Op cit*
29. *Motor Cycle*, 17 June 1978
30. Charlie Williams, conversation with author
31. *Motor Cycle News*, 12 June 1979
32. Williams, p.157
33. *Motor Cycle News*, 4 June 1980
34. Charlie Williams, conversation with author
35. *Motor Cycle News*, 11 June 1980
36. Grant, p.223
37. *Motor Cycle News*, 11 June 1980
38. *Liverpool Echo*, 6 June 1981
39. *Liverpool Daily Post*, 5 June 1981

Chapter Five: Sidecar Success, 1974–1981

1. Kenny Arthur, conversation with author
2. George O'Dell, *Sidecar Championship*, London, 1978, p.81
3. O'Dell, p.82
4. Kenny Arthur, conversation with author
5. Kenny Arthur, conversation with author
6. O'Dell, p.86
7. www.dickgreasley.com
8. *Motor Cycle News*, 10 June 1981
9. *Op cit*

BIBLIOGRAPHY

Barker, Stuart, *Tourist Trophy Century*, London, 2007
Bennett, Greg, *Yamaha Two Stroke Production Roadracing Motorcycles Volume 1: 1959 to 1982*, Australia, 2002
Duff, Michelle, *The Mike Duff Story: Make Haste Slowly*, Toronto, 1999
Gowenlock, Roger, *Yamaha's Glorious Grand Prix History*, NL, 2009
Grant, Mick, *Roadracing*, London, 1979
Grant, Mick, *Takin' the Mick*, Yeovil, 2012
Macauley, Ted, *Mike the Bike – Again*, Dorchester, 2018
Macauley, Ted, *The Yamaha Legend*, New York, 1979
MacKellar, Colin, *Yamaha Two-Stroke Twins*, Osprey, 1985
McDiarmid, Mac, *Joey Dunlop: His Authorised Biography*, Yeovil, 2001
O'Dell, George and Beacham, Ian, *Sidecar Championship*, London, 1978
Peck, Alan, *No Time to Lose – The Fast Moving World of Bill Ivy*, London, 1972
Read, Phil, *Rebel Read: The Prince of Speed*, Malta, 2014
Robb, Tommy, *TT to Tokyo*, Douglas, 1974
Taveri, Luigi, *Mein Leben auf Zwei Rädern*, Stuttgart, 1969
Williams, Charlie, *It was the Best of Times*, NL, 2019

INDEX

Agostini, Giacomo, 21, 44, 70, 76, 79, 84, 90, 115, 122
All Japan Autobike Endurance Road Race, 12
Amano, Chiyomaru, 10
Anderson, Hugh, 21, 39, 44
Angel, Samuel 'Sonny', 16
Anscheidt, Hans George, 48
Arthur, Kenny, 133, 135, 137–40, 142, 145

BMW, 18, 133, 151
BSA-Triumph, 86, 134, 144
Ballacraine, 46, 66, 79, 96, 99, 109–11, 121, 129–30
Ballaugh Bridge, 82, 96, 99, 101, 109–10, 130, 138, 141, 143, 148
Bartol, Harald, 65, 122, 124
Biggs, Vince, 149
Biland, Rolf, 144
Birch, Kenny, 143
Black Hut, 147
Boddice, Mick, 144, 148–9
Boughey, Roy, 32
Braddan Bridge, 114

Brandywell, 77
Bray Hill, 30–1, 35, 69, 97, 107, 126, 130, 144
Broad, Ted, 125–6
Brouwer, Ferry, 73
Brown, Gerald, 100
Bryans, Ralph, 46, 48–9, 56, 108
Bungalow, 80, 99, 101, 110, 118
Burns, Mick, 137

Cannell, Geoff, 82, 99
Carpenter, Phil, 95–6
Carruthers, Kel, 66–7, 102
Catalina Grand Prix, 14
Chatterton, Derek, 74
Chatterton, Mike, 49
Cheney, Eric, 73
Cooper, John, 33
Creg-ny-Baa, 39, 60, 77, 93, 112, 138
Cronk y Voddy, 49, 127, 138
Cycle World, 77

DKW, 11
Daytona, 102
Degner, Ernst, 21

Dongen, Cees van, 91
Dugdale, Alan, 76, 90–1, 96
Duff, Mike, 26, 29–31, 33–41, 43–8
Dunlop, Joey, 103, 113–14, 121, 128–31
Dunlop tyres, 57, 130

FIM, 51–2, 54–5, 62, 64, 89
Farmer, Bob, 49
Fath, Helmut, 73
First World War, 10
Fogarty, George, 120
Formula 750, 70, 85, 87, 89–90, 96, 131

George, Alex, 99, 103, 105, 107, 109–10, 124, 129
Gilera, 24
Giron, Luis, 18
Glen Helen, 117
Godfrey, Tony, 21–3, 26–7
Goodyear tyres, 137
Gooseneck, 46, 141
Gould, Rodney, 57, 59, 66–8, 71, 74, 115
Governor's Bridge, 32, 40, 59, 71, 94, 138, 142
Graham, Jacky, 129
Graham, Stuart, 48
Grant, Mick, 67, 70, 72, 81–4, 90, 93–8, 101, 106–107, 109, 111–12, 114–15, 119–21, 128–30

Greasley, Dick, 133, 140–3, 148
Guthrie, Billy, 103

Hailwood, Mike, 18, 41, 44–5, 47–53, 56, 58, 72, 101, 115–21, 124, 129
Hamamatsu, 9, 14, 18, 33, 36, 85
Hanks, Roy, 149
Hartle, John, 26
Hawthorne pub, 126
Hasegawa, Hiroshi, 19, 21
Hasegawa, Takehiko, 32–3, 39
Hata, Noriyuki, 14–15, 19
Hennen, Pat, 117
Herron, Tom, 99–100, 105–11, 114
Highlander, 31, 35
Higley, Frank, 34
Hobson, Mac, 133, 137, 143–4
Hocking, Gary, 18
Hokkaido, 10
Honda Motor Company, 14–15, 18–23, 25, 27–8, 31–2, 38, 40–1, 44, 48, 51, 53, 56, 62, 104, 116, 128, 130–1, 151
Honda, Soichiro, 15
Huggett, Ken, 82

Ireson, Trevor, 148
Itoh, Fumio, 14, 16, 18–19, 21–7, 31
Itoh, Mitsuo, 21
Ivy, Bill, 33–5, 37, 39, 41–4, 46–51, 53–61, 68, 122, 151

Jefferies, Tony, 70
Johansson, Bengt-Goran (Benga), 145–50

Kalauch, Wolfgang, 140
Katayama, Yoshimo, 48
Katayama, Takizuma, 108–109
Kate's Cottage, 39, 138
Kawakami, Gen-Ichi, 11–13, 53
Kawakami, Kaichi, 10
Kawasaki Motors, 97–8, 101, 109, 111, 119
Keaney, Danny, 79, 89, 97

Länsivuori, Tepi, 101
Liverpool Echo, 113

MV Agusta, 15, 20, 40–1, 70, 76
MZ, 15, 21, 41, 49, 71
Macauley, Ted, 115, 121
Masuko, Osamu, 18–19
Maxton Engineering, 80–1, 87, 90, 94, 98, 105, 112, 122, 124, 127
Milntown, 23, 58
Minter, Derek, 26
Mitsui Yamaha, 124–5, 127
Mortimer, Chas, 68–9, 71, 75, 79, 89–90, 92–9, 103–107, 112, 116, 119, 122–3
Motohashi, Akiyasu, 49
Motor Cycle Mechanics, 82
Motor Cycle News, 52, 76, 147
Mount Fuji Ascent, 12

Mountain Mile, 37, 46, 59
Musical instruments, 9–10, 12, 24, 97

Naito, Hiroshi, 14–15, 19, 23
Naito, Masaharu, 33, 56–7
Nippon Gakki Corporation 9–11, 13
Noguchi, Taneharu, 16, 18
Norton Motors, 21, 49, 64–6, 70, 75, 77, 91

O'Dell, George, 133–6, 139–40, 142–3
Offenstadt, Éric, 64–5, 101
Oishi, Hideo, 18–19

Padgetts of Batley, 66
Parlotti, Gilberto, 75–6
Perris, Frank, 21
Potter, Dave, 125
Priest, Bob, 92, 101

Quarry Bends, 74, 138, 149
Quarter Bridge, 18, 30–1, 68, 100, 144

Ramsey, 23, 31, 46, 60, 75, 79–80, 82, 100, 110, 114, 130, 141
Rea, John, 104, 128
Read, Phil, 23–30, 32–42, 45–6, 48–53, 55–61, 66, 68, 70–6, 84, 90, 111, 121, 151
Redman, Jim, 21–3, 25, 27, 31, 36–7, 40–1, 56

Rhencullen, 35
Robb, Tommy, 21, 31, 69–70, 79–80, 99, 122
Roberts, Eddie, 98, 112–14
Roberts, Kenny, 67, 88, 116
Robinson, Donny, 128, 131
Rutter, Tony, 65–6, 76, 81–2, 90, 92–3, 97, 99, 101, 104–105, 107, 109–10

Sarah's Cottage, 75
Schoolhouse Corner, 46, 60
Second World War, 11
Seeley, Colin, 64–5, 73, 104, 113
Sheene, Barry, 68–9, 93–4, 100
Sheene, Frank, 68
Shepherd, Alan, 26
Signpost Corner, 60
Simpson, Bill, 103, 110–11
Skeels, Mick, 140, 142
Smith, Barry, 131
Smith, Bill, 49, 69, 102, 127
Sports Motorcycles, 115, 120
Sprayson, Ken, 48
Steinhausen, Rolf, 140, 144
Strikes, 10, 24
Sulby Bridge, 44
Sulby Straight, 18, 35, 74, 107, 138, 148–9
Sunako, Yoshikasa, 18, 21
Suzuki, Kaneyoshi, 26
Suzuki Motors, 17, 19–21, 27, 38–9, 44, 56, 62, 68, 109, 111, 131

Tait, Percy, 21, 101–102
Tanaka-san, 68
Taylor, Jock, 134, 144–50
Takei (chief of research), 13
Taveri, Luigi, 40, 46–7
Tokyo earthquake (1923), 10
Trachsel, Ernst, 144
Trollope, Dennis, 146–7
Tuxworth, Neil, 109
Two-stroke technology, 11–12, 15–17, 20, 24, 27, 31, 35–6, 63, 65–6, 71, 77, 85, 102, 108, 118, 121, 125, 134–5, 140, 142, 151–2

Walker, Murray, 22, 28, 38, 40, 44
Ward, Lewis, 145
Williams, Charlie, 69, 76–7, 79–81, 90–8, 100–101, 105–12, 119, 122–7, 131
Williams, Donnie, 148
Williams, John, 80, 82, 95, 97, 100–101, 105–107, 109, 111–12, 115, 121
Williams, Peter, 71–2
Windle, Terry, 134–6, 142–3, 146–7
Windy Corner, 72, 128
Woodman, Derek, 49
Woods, Stanley, 49, 109

Yamaha models
  AS2, 64
  LC350, 127
  LD350, 127

OW31, 88
R3, 64
RA31A, 84
RA41, 17
RA55, 19
RA75, 19–20
RA97, 39
RD05, 33
RDO5A, 48, 84
RD48, 15, 17, 19
RD56, 15, 19–20, 25, 27–8, 32, 64
RD250, 103
RD350, 78
RD400, 91, 103
TD1, 63
TD1-B, 63
TD2, 64, 66–7, 73, 77
TD3, 80
TDB2, 64
TE1, 63
TR2, 91
TR3 77
TZ250, 78, 115
TZ250C 106
TZ250F, 123
TZ250G, 127–8
TZ350, 77–8, 82, 88, 90, 103–104, 115, 124
TZ750, 85–7, 102, 115, 133
TZ750A, 102
TZ750B, 87
TZ750C, 88
TZ750D, 88
TZ750E, 120
YA-1 (Akatombo), 11–12, 14
YA-2, 12
YDS-1, 12
YDS-2, 63
YX18, 15
YX48, 18
YZ263, 64, 67
YZ263A, 64
YZR500 OW20, 84–6
Yamaha Motor Company, 11, 13, 15, 20, 23–4, 27–8, 34, 40–1, 48, 53, 55–6, 61–3, 67, 70, 84, 97, 115, 131, 151
Yamaha, Torakusu, 9–10